D1038572

PHOTOGRAPHY
AND THE LAW

ISBN 0-8174-0479-1

Photography
and the Law

BY
GEORGE CHERNOFF
AND
HERSHEL SARBIN

Fourth Edition

AMPHOTO
American Photographic Book Publishing Co., Inc.
NEW YORK

KF2042
,P45
C44
1971

770

C524

Copyright © 1958, 1965, 1967, 1971
by George Chernoff and Hershel Sarbin

Library of Congress Catalog Card Number 74-133888

Published in New York by American Photographic Book Publishing Co.,
Inc. All rights reserved. No part of this book may be reproduced in any
form or by any means without permission in writing by the publisher.

Manufactured in the United States of America

Foreword

THIS FOURTH EDITION of *Photography and the Law* reflects the influence of social changes over the past few years. The advent of the sex revolution, the age of sexual permissiveness, the emphasis on free speech and free press in times of protest over the war in Southeast Asia and social injustices at home all have had their impact on the courts.

These changes will be especially noticeable in the area of obscenity and right of privacy portions of this book.

It is virtually impossible for a photographer not to be confronted at times with legal problems that affect practically every phase of his work — from the moment he clicks the shutter of his camera and has to determine whether the subject may be properly photographed, to the time he receives the finished picture and has to decide where and how it can be used.

Regardless of whether he be an amateur or professional, he should have sufficient understanding of the law applicable to photography to enable him to recognize the existence of a legal problem and obtain legal advice or assistance before any damage is done.

Photography is one of the few fields that has not been flooded with books explaining its legal aspects. True, articles have been written from time to time on different subjects relating to the law of photography, but the need has been great for a good book treating all legal aspects under one cover. This book is designed to fill that need. It should be a very valuable part of the photographer's equipment.

THE AUTHORS

JUN 14 1971

Contents

Introduction

THROUGH THE YEARS during which the authors have written a column on legal problems for *Popular Photography*, our readers have often asked: Where can we find — in one place — the answers to all our questions about the legal aspects of photography? This book represents our attempt to supply a satisfactory answer to that question — to provide the photographer with a basic guide and simple analysis of those areas of the law with which he is most concerned.

In a real sense, any book concerning the law must fall short of the ultimate goal of stating precisely what the law is, for the law cannot be set forth in A B C order as a simple set of rules. It is more complex than that. Moreover, social, political and economic change is accompanied by a continuous refinement and shaping of law to meet current conditions. The reader should bear in mind that any book written for laymen about the law must contain some over-simplification if it is not to be so comprehensive and complex that it becomes useless as a guide. We have tried to organize this book and select our material with this in mind.

The first problem — and one which seems to puzzle many amateur photographers — is: Can I snap the shutter of my camera wherever and whenever I please? Can a policeman stop me from taking a picture of a street brawl? Can the guard at a museum prevent me from using flash? Can I take a picture of a battleship or of a military installation? And since taking the picture seems to be a good beginning, this is where we have started.

From there we have moved, in Chapter 2, to the use one may make of a picture, for this is a problem that should be considered almost simultaneously with the snapping of the shutter. Thus, in Chapter 2 the problem of invasion of privacy is covered. We have also discussed when a photographer must have a model release, and what kind of a release it should be.

In Chapter 3 we have moved to ownership, for many of the problems of use are intertwined with the problem of who owns the picture.

When pictures are started on their way to the processor, and perhaps later to a prospective publisher, another group of problems is encountered. What happens if the processor damages the film? Or if it is lost in transit? How can one protect himself against loss of valuable pictures? And is it possible to prove that a picture has a specific value? This is the subject matter of Chapter 4.

Chapter 5 deals with the nude in photography and the law of obscenity. This problem has two distinct levels. The basic, underlying problem is whether the photograph of a nude may be considered art. Where is the line drawn between obscenity and art? Motion pictures as well as photographs in books and magazines are considered in this area. The second problem—a very practical one —involves the manner in which the Post Office and the processor deal with pictures of nudes.

We have already noted that when a picture is to be published, the law of privacy and the model release assume great importance. Chapters 6 and 7 cover two further problems of publication — copyright and libel. How does the photographer copyright his pictures? At what cost? What is the extent of his protection? When *must* a picture be copyrighted? These, and a host of other questions, are answered in Chapter 6. In the following chapter we deal with problems of libel — problems which generally arise from distortions in the photograph or improper captions.

The use of the photograph as evidence in the courtroom has always been an interesting subject, although most photographers are not directly concerned with its problems. Chapter 8 is an introduction to this subject.

Finally, Chapter 9 covers the subject of the status of photography and the statutes requiring photographers to secure licenses. Whether photography is to be classified as a profession, an art or a trade is often an important question when matters of local and state taxation are involved, and it is well for all photographers to be aware of the efforts which have been made from time to time to require licenses.

The authors feel compelled to state once more that the book is intended as a guide to photographers, not as the source of conclusive answers to all their legal problems. Legal advice must, in the final analysis, be obtained from one's own lawyer.

The authors would like to express their appreciation to Stanley A. Katcher for reviewing the manuscript of the first edition in its entirety and for writing a foreword to the book.

The authors are particularly grateful to Miss Judith Grad, who has made a major contribution to the revised edition. Miss Grad is a graduate of the New York University School of Law, Associate Editor of the Bulletin of the Copyright Society of the U.S.A., and an associate in the law firm of Rosen, Seton & Sarbin. She is also a member of the Committees on Copyright Revision and International Copyright of the Section of Patent Trademark and Copyright Law of the American Bar Association.

We also wish to thank Theodore R. Kupferman and E. Gabriel Perle of the New York Bar, who have generously taken the time to appraise and evaluate various chapters in the book.

This is the fourth edition of *Photography and the Law*. The previous editions were so well received by those in the photographic field and by those interested in the law applicable to photography that the authors deemed it worthwhile to bring the book up to date, especially in view of the important changes in certain aspects of the law, notably in the area of obscenity.

In the hope that this book will continue to serve as a valuable contribution to the field of photography, we have taken the time and effort to prepare this revised edition.

CHAPTER I

Taking The Picture

A PHOTOGRAPHER'S CAMERA is almost always with him — at home, on the street, in the theatre, or at a museum. And his right to use that camera wherever he may be is essentially unrestrained. Nevertheless, there are a few rules restricting the use of cameras, both as to place and subject matter, which every photographer should know. In reading this chapter it is important for the photographer to distinguish between the right to take a picture and the right to use that picture. This chapter is concerned only with the right to take a picture. The right to use it is covered elsewhere in this book.

One general limitation that always applies to the right to take a picture is that the photographer must not commit a nuisance or interfere with others when taking a picture. With this in mind, let us examine the specific places and subject matter to which restrictions might apply.

PICTURES IN THE STUDIO

The only restrictions applicable to taking pictures in the studio are those which might apply to any business, and these — such matters as Sunday laws and negligence — are either specifically covered by local ordinance or are matters of general legal knowledge, and are therefore not within the scope of this work. (See pp. 129-134 with respect to license requirements for professional photographers.)

A word of caution should be spoken, however, concerning the application of the rules of negligence to photographic studios.

People who come into the studio or into your home, if you are using
it for picture-taking purposes, are invitees, and you must provide
reasonably safe quarters for them. The requirement is well illus-
trated by a case in which a child, while being photographed, was
severely burned when he came in contact with exposed steam pipes
next to the table.

In ruling that damages should be paid for the injury alone, the
court declared: *

> ... the owner and tenant cooperated in creating a condition which
> any reasonable, prudent person must have known could cause injury.
> The anticipated use of the room, its ineffective lighting, the harmless
> appearance of the pipe, its potential capacity to severely burn, if
> contacted when full of steam, the possibility that young children
> would be present in the room and come in contact with the pipe,
> were matters which a reasonable prudent person would have con-
> sidered.[1]

PICTURES IN THE STREET

Outside of the possibility of an occasional local ordinance
restricting the taking of pictures on a public street, the photographer's right to take pictures on public streets and highways is
clear, so long as he does not interfere with traffic.

The problem here is actually somewhat the reverse, for there
are times when individuals try by physical assault to prevent a
photographer from taking a picture. In such instances, the courts
have generally stepped in to protect the photographer's right to
take pictures in a public place. Some years ago New York State
even made it unlawful to injure the apparatus of a news photographer engaged in the pursuit of his occupation in a public place
or gathering.[2]

IN THE THEATRE, MUSEUM, OR PLACE OF AMUSEMENT

It seems quite clear that a museum can establish its own rules
and regulations for the taking of pictures. Some museums simply
prohibit any use of photographic equipment. Others will not allow
flash or tripods.

*See list of citations page 149.

Theatres, sports arenas, or other places of amusement may, if they wish, also restrict the use of cameras.

PHOTOGRAPHING MONEY OR SECURITIES

The laws of the United States Government, until a few years ago, made it a criminal act to photograph any "obligation or security of the United States."[3] This included bonds, certificates of indebtedness, coupons and deposit certificates, as well as all kinds of U.S. paper currency. Photographing paper money or other "obligations or securities of the United States" is still restricted, but is no longer absolutely forbidden.

The law[4] now provides that black and white photographs of such "obligations or securities" may be taken and reproduced for "philatelic, numismatic, educational, historical or newsworthy purposes." This list of purposes is fairly broad, and considerable picture-taking can be fitted within its limits. But the use of such photographs for advertising (except for the "legitimate" advertising of qualified numismatic and philatelic dealers) is specifically forbidden. Color motion pictures, slides and microfilms may also be made for the purposes listed above, but you cannot make prints or other reproductions of these color photographs without special permission from the Secretary of the Treasury. Photographing a *portion* of an obligation or security of the United States is subject to the same restrictions as photographing the *whole*.

As compared with the former harsh law, the present restrictions are more in line with the actual government purpose of preventing counterfeiting. A violation of this more liberal law, however, is *still a criminal offense*. Although a first offender who unwittingly violated the law might expect to be let off with a warning and seizure of the offending photograph, any repetition of the offense would probably meet with drastic action.

Since the specific language of the prohibitory statute speaks of reproductions "in the likeness of" obligations of the United States, it is conceivable that one might photograph paper money so that no part of the money is "in the likeness" of genuine money. The distance of the camera from the object, the particular angle at which the photograph is taken, or the sharpness of focus, might avoid the degree of "likeness" which would constitute a violation of the law. The safe way to avoid a violation, of course, is simply not to photograph obligations or securities of the United States except in the manner and for the purposes which the law permits.

Before 1951 the Federal law prohibited illustrations of coins, but in that year an amendment was adopted which removed the restrictions on photographs and printed illustrations of coins.[5]

The penal laws of some states prohibit or restrict the photographing of stocks, bonds and other securities as well as all instruments for the payment of money.[6]

POSTAGE STAMPS

The Federal law places exactly the same restrictions on the photographing of postage stamps, U.S. and foreign, as it does on photographing of money.[7]

The Attorney General of the United States, however, has given an opinion that restrictions on postage stamp illustrations do not apply to demonetized stamps of foreign countries — that is, stamps issued by governments no longer in existence or foreign stamps which are not valid as postage in the country of origin. Such stamps may be photographed and published without restriction as to purpose or use of color.

MISCELLANEOUS

During World War II the President of the United States, acting under his right to declare that certain vital military and naval installations required protection against dissemination of information, ruled out the taking of any photograph of military and naval installations and equipment without obtaining permission of the proper authorities.[8] This power may be invoked at any time, and it is well for photographers to be aware of its broad scope.

The law also says that citizenship certificates may not be the subject of a photograph.[9] Bills of lading are subject to restrictions since they could easily be offered as genuine bills of lading. If one knowingly and with intent to defraud photographs any bill of lading purporting to represent goods, such action is a misdemeanor.[10]

THE COURTROOM

One of the most controversial subjects affecting photography to come before the courts in recent years involves the application of Canon 35, a rule promulgated by the American Bar Association many years ago restricting the taking of photographs in the courtroom. Canon 35 stated:

> Proceedings in court should be conducted with fitting dignity and decorum. The taking of photographs in the courtroom, during sessions of the court or recesses between sessions, and the broadcasting or televising of court proceedings *[are calculated to]* *detract from the essential dignity of the proceedings, distract the witness from giving his testimony, degrade the court, and create misconceptions with respect thereto in the mind of the public* and should not be permitted. (Italics added.)

The language of Canon 35 is harsh and strict, and all the efforts of the National Press Photographers' Association and others to secure a revision in the rule have resulted to date in only a minor change in wording. In 1963, the words in brackets above were removed by vote of the House of Delegates of the American Bar Association. Obviously, although the language is now a little more restrained, the effect of Canon 35 is completely undisturbed by this small change.

We quote from the report of this action which appeared in the *American Bar News* (an official publication of the American Bar Association) for February 15, 1963:

> A decade or more of controversy over Canon 35 was climaxed by the vote by which the House voiced a resounding "no" to proposals that Canon 35 be modified to allow photographing and broadcasting of trials. The House agreed with the findings of a special A.B.A. study committee that, despite gains in photo and broadcasting technology, the paraphernalia of these media in courtrooms tends to be disruptive of a normal judicial atmosphere and to jeopardize the right to a fair trial.

This statement seems strange. There was a time, indeed, when the taking of photographs in a courtroom could well be said to create a disturbing influence. Times have changed, however. Today the camera is a much more unobtrusive recorder than it was when Canon 35 came into being many years ago.

During the course of an investigation of New York State trotting tracks a few years ago, a newspaper photographer was ejected from the hearing room when it was discovered that he was taking pictures with a concealed 35mm camera. He had been taking the pictures for two and one half days without affecting the decorum of the courtroom. Despite the fact that he had taken over 30 pictures of political figures as they were testifying, no one had noticed the camera work.

In the face of such evidence it is difficult for us, and for photographers generally, to understand the continued vitality of Canon 35. The 1963 change, as can be seen from the American Bar News report, is really a reaffirmation of the rule. Much of the difficulty, especially in recent years, arises from the fact that discussion of Canon 35 has so often centered on the courtroom disturbance which can be caused by television broadcasting, without sufficient separate consideration being given to photography as such.

One interesting case involving Canon 35 took place in Cleveland, Ohio, when three staff members of *The Cleveland Press* were convicted of contempt of court for taking a picture at the arraignment of a prisoner charged with embezzlement. The judge had told newsmen that no pictures were to be taken, and the attorney for the defendant quoted the judge as saying, ". . . the ban had been imposed because otherwise he would be disciplined by the Cleveland Bar Association."

The newspaper's position was well stated by Mr. Louis B. Seltzer, editor of the *Press,* who said:

> It is our basic argument, apart from the direct issue involved, that photographic science has made picture taking in a courtroom beyond the claim that it distracts or intrudes on the proceedings in a courtroom, and is essentially no different than a reporter covering a trial with his pencil and pad.
>
> It is the further contention that under a broad interpretation of the constitutional guaranty of a free press in this democracy that the people's right to know endows the free press not only with ears to write but eyes to illustrate modern court proceedings.

Mr. Seltzer's argument did not prevail, however, and the Appellate Court in Ohio supported the judge's ruling. The Court said in part:

> The rules of courtroom conduct must be such as to remove it from the distractions and disturbances of the market place, and to maintain as nearly as possible an atmosphere conducive to profound and undisturbed deliberation . . . The flashlight inevitably startles those nearby when used without notice. Its use is not conducive to sustained mental effort. If a photographer can take one picture he can take two or a dozen.[12]

In reaching its decision the Court cited a Supreme Court case which gave the State and Federal Courts "the power to protect themselves from disorders and disturbances in the Courtroom."

In many states, Canon 35 is strictly observed throughout the state, on occasion even being extended to local rules forbidding the taking of photographs in courtroom corridors, or even on the courtroom steps. Generally, taking photographs outside the actual courtroom is permitted. In some states, Texas for example, the observance of Canon 35 depends on the discretion of the individual judge. Thus, for example, Judge Joe B. Brown permitted *television cameras* in the courtroom when the jury returned its verdict in the Jack Ruby trial in Dallas, but did not permit television *broadcasting* or the taking of still photographs during the actual trial.[13] In Colorado, which has modified Canon 35, no witness or juror can be photographed or broadcast over his express objection. In New York, by statute, Sec. 52, Civil Rights Law, the taking of moving pictures, televising and broadcasting are forbidden in the courtroom.

Although a few words offensive to photographers were removed from Canon 35, it seems to us that over recent years there has been a net loss rather than a net gain to photographers in this connection because of the increasing number of states in which there is a statewide rule forbidding any picture taking in any courtroom, leaving the judge without discretion to grant permission to a photographer to take pictures.

Despite the universally severe criticism of Canon 35 among photographers, we have always noted in discussing the subject with them that they recognize the inherent right of a judge to control the conduct of a trial over which he is presiding, and the necessity of maintaining order in the courtroom. We believe that a judge should be considered competent to do this, and that he should not be compelled by Canon 35 to forbid courtroom photography in situations where he does not believe that courtroom decorum would be disturbed.

CHAPTER II

Right Of Privacy

EVERY PHOTOGRAPHER who plans to sell, publish or exhibit his pictures must acquire some knowledge concerning the law of privacy and model releases. In this chapter it is our purpose to show you when and under what circumstances you will need a model release, and when you will be reasonably safe without one.

Whenever a photographer sells or exhibits a picture of a living person[1] he runs the risk of being sued for invasion of the right of privacy. In fact, the greatest number of lawsuits brought against photographers today is in this area. What is the right of privacy? Generally, the courts have said that it is the right of a person to be let alone, to be free from undeserved and undesired publicity. It has also been described as the right to live one's life in seclusion, without being subjected to unwarranted publicity.

This does not mean that the mere taking of a person's picture is of itself necessarily an invasion of privacy. Obviously, the public has a right to many types of knowledge that would be cut off if the definition we have used were taken too literally. In the years since the right of privacy was first recognized, the courts of the land have attempted to strike a proper balance between the individual's right to be let alone and the public's broad right to knowledge and information.

In attempting to strike this balance, the courts and state legislatures have uniformly looked to the use to which a picture or a person's name was put. Some states have said the prohibited use was one "for advertising or trade purposes." Others have merely said that privacy is invaded when the name or picture of a person is used in a way which offends the sensibilities of an ordinary person. We shall see later how the courts have refined and shaped these broad concepts to accommodate the needs of both public and individual.

If a photographer could get a release from every person of age who turns up in his pictures (and from the parents of every person not of age), he would have no problems with right-of-privacy suits. Getting a release, however, is not always easy and is a chore most people prefer to avoid. That is why it is absolutely essential to know when a release is necessary, and this requires some additional knowledge about the right of privacy.

HISTORY

Although the earliest intimations of this legal right can be traced back to ancient Jewish law, the concept of an enforceable right of privacy as we know it today dates from 1890. In that year, in an article in the *Harvard Law Review*,[2] Louis Brandeis (later Justice Brandeis) and Samuel D. Warren argued for recognition by the courts of the right of people to be secure in their private lives from interference by the press and undeserved publicity.

Almost simultaneously the courts were hearing cases in which an effort was made to invoke a right of privacy, and in some instances the complaining parties were successful.[3] But in 1902, in the now famous case of *Roberson v. Rochester Folding Box Co.*,[4] the right of privacy suffered a severe blow at the hands of the highest court in the State of New York. The case involved the appearance of posters and magazine advertisements for "Franklin Mills Flour" which were adorned with the photograph of a comely lass named Roberson. The purpose was to show that both Miss Roberson and the flour were of excellent quality and to entice the reader to at least try the product. Miss Roberson objected to the undesired publicity and sued for damages.

The court, however, did not come to the aid of the aggrieved Miss Roberson. Instead, it denied the existence of the right of privacy and held that no legal right had been violated. This decision resulted in a storm of criticism by the press, as well as general popular disapproval, and at the very next session of the New York State Legislature there was enacted into law a right of privacy.

The New York statute (reprinted at the end of this chapter) became the model for similar statutes in several other states, but the development of the right of privacy in this country has largely been by rule of court rather than by statute. At the present time the right of privacy has been held by the courts to exist in Alabama, Arizona, Arkansas, California, Colorado, Connecticut, Delaware, District of Columbia, Florida, Georgia, Idaho, Illinois, Indiana, Iowa, Kansas, Kentucky, Louisiana, Michigan, Missouri, Montana, New Jersey, North Carolina, Ohio, Oregon, Pennsylvania, South Carolina, South Dakota and West Virginia.

Still other states have followed the lead of New York in enacting statutes protecting the right of privacy. Such legislation has been enacted in Utah,[5] Virginia,[6] Wisconsin,[7] Oklahoma and Nebraska, although the prohibition of the Wisconsin statute merely applied to the publication (except as may be necessary in the institution or prosecution of a criminal proceeding) of the name of a woman who may have been raped or subjected to criminal assault. The Utah and Virginia statutes essentially follow the New York statute.

Despite the growth of the right of privacy during the last sixty years, it must be remembered that the doctrine is still very much in its infancy. The outlines of its nature and extent as sketched in judicial decisions are still rough and difficult to define. In many states even the existence of the right of privacy is still an undetermined question. For this reason the writer in this area of law hesitates to make broad, sweeping pronouncements concerning the status of the law of privacy.

We have already pointed out that in New York, by statute, a person's name or likeness may not be used for "advertising or trade" purposes without written consent. In states not having a statute similar to New York's, the courts inquire whether a particular use is offensive to the sensibilities of an ordinary person. The language used in the cases may be different, but with few exceptions the courts in the states where the right of privacy is recognized have arrived at similar results on similar sets of facts. In broad terms, the courts have applied the right of privacy to prevent unwarranted exploitation of one's personality without his consent.[8]

THE LAHIRI CASE

In 1937 a right of privacy action was brought in the courts of New York by a professional Hindu musician as the result of the publication of a story in a New York newspaper concerning the "rope trick" performed by plaintiff.[9] The plaintiff's picture had been used to illustrate the story and he claimed an invasion of his privacy which violated the New York statute. Justice Shientag, in deciding that Lahiri's privacy had not been invaded, formulated four rules concerning the use of photographs to illustrate articles which have been applied by the courts of New York ever since and which are also cited by courts in other jurisdictions. The rules were summarized by Judge Hofstadter of the New York Supreme Court this way:

(1) Recovery under the statute may be had, if the photograph is published in or as part of an advertisement, or for advertising purposes;

(2) Recovery may be had, if the photograph is used in connection with a work of fiction;

(3) No recovery may be had if the photograph is published in connection with an article of current news or immediate public interest; and

(4) No recovery may be had, as a general rule, if the article is educational or informative in character.[10]

As to the last two categories, however, the courts have said that there may be an invasion of privacy "if the photograph used has so tenuous a connection with the news item or educational article that it can be said to have no legitimate relation to it and be used for the purpose of promoting the sale of the publication;[11] or, as the courts have said, if the use is such that it would be "repugnant to one's sense of decency," or would "outrage common ordinary decency."[12] Now let us see how the courts have applied the rules.

ADVERTISING

The courts have usually had little difficulty in deciding what constitutes a use for "advertising purposes." Clearly, the display of a photograph in connection with the endorsement of a product is such a use. For example, where a woman paid a photographer to make a portrait of her, and the photographer, without the subject's consent, sold a copy of the portrait to a publisher who used it to promote the sale of a book on hair culture, a New York court said that the picture had been used for advertising purposes.[13] Thus, the determination by the photographer as to whether a picture is being used for advertising purposes is, in most cases, not a difficult task.

An interesting question arises, however, when a picture originally exempt from restrictions against invasion of privacy because it was a legitimate news picture used as such is republished for advertising purposes. A good illustration of the special rule here is the recent case of *Booth v. Curtis Publishing Co.*[14] *Holiday* magazine published a picture of actress Shirley Booth in a legitimate news article to which the picture was clearly relevant. Miss Booth did not complain about this original use, but when the picture was republished in advertisements for *Holiday* which appeared in the *New Yorker* and *Advertising Age,* she sued *Holiday's* publisher, claiming that her picture and name had been used for advertising and/or purposes of trade without her consent. The court, however, agreed with the defendant's argument that using news pictures to *advertise the publication in which they first appeared* is merely "incidental" to the privilege of using news pictures for legitimate news purposes, and comes within the same exemption.

In pointing out the difference between use of a news picture in "incidental" advertising of the news medium, and its use in "collateral" advertising, advertising of a product which has no direct connection with the magazine or newspaper in which the picture first appeared, the court in the *Booth* case discussed the case of *Flores v. Mosler Safe Co.,*[15] which had come up in New York a few years earlier. The court said this was a good example of "collateral" use of a news picture which constituted an invasion of privacy for which a plaintiff could recover. In this case, the Mosler Safe Company distributed a circular on which it reproduced, as a dramatic illustration of the danger to unprotected business records in case of fire, a striking picture of a burning building, together with the captions and news story which had accompanied the picture when it was originally published in a newspaper. The story made several references to the plaintiff. The court in that case held that although the material reproduced, both picture and story, was originally legitimate news material, it did not come within the "news" exemption to uses for advertising because the circular advertised safes rather than the newspaper which had published the story. The same rule would apply to similar use of a picture of a person (rather than a building) without the necessity of the additional use of the person's name.

Gautier v. Pro Football, Inc.[16] is an illustration of a case in which the New York Court of Appeals was asked to determine the application of the term "advertising purposes" to an unusual situation, and in which, as in the *Holiday* magazine case, it decided that there had been no violation of the Civil Rights Law.

In this case the plaintiff, a well-known trainer of animals, performed before an audience of 35,000 persons between the halves of a professional football game. He had not given his consent to the telecast of his performance, but the entire football game, including his performance, was in fact televised. In the course of the telecast paid commercial announcements for Chesterfield cigarettes were made. There was one such commercial just before plaintiff's performance, and another just after his performance. Plaintiff urged that on the foregoing facts, his name and picture had been used for advertising purposes in violation of Sections 50 and 51 of the Civil Rights Law. The Court of Appeals affirmed the Appellate Division's decision that there had been no use of plaintiff's name or picture for advertising purposes. The court pointed out that although the telecast was paid for by Chesterfield, the entire program was not thereby constituted a solicitation for patronage. The court said that "unless plaintiff's name or picture were in some way connected with the 'commercial,' the mere fact of sponsorship of the telecast would not . . . suffice to violate the statute in this respect."

In line with the *Booth v. Curtis Publishing Co.* case above, permitting the use of news pictures to advertise the publication in which they first appeared and calling such use "incidental" to the privilege of publishing news pictures for legitimate news purposes, another interesting case was decided in March, 1969, when an advertising use was held permissible by a publisher without the consent of the person involved. In *Rand v. Hearst Corp.,* 298 N.Y.S. 2d 405, the Appellate Division of the New York Supreme Court was called upon to decide at what point a public figure (in this case a well-known author) might complain when her style of writing was compared with that of another author and this comparison appeared on the cover of the other author's book. The court, in deciding that not every advertising use is prohibited, said:

> The law—narrowly written—attempts to do so by proscribing the use of the person's name or picture for the purposes of trade or advertising. However, it has already been clearly established that not in every instance where a person's picture or name is used in connection with advertising will a violation of the statute be found. (See *Booth v. Curtis Publishing Co.,* supra.) The *Booth* case presented a situation where a person's photograph was used for advertising purposes and yet it was held that plaintiff had no cause of action.
>
> [6] Thus, in construing the law, the courts have looked to its underlying purpose—the need it was intended to fill—and rather than adhering to its exact letter have interpreted the spirit in which it was written. The words "advertising purposes" and for the "purposes of trade" were used as the means to carry out the law's fundamental purpose—the protection of an individual's right of privacy. They must be construed narrowly and not used to curtail the right of free speech, or free press, or to shut off the publication of matters newsworthy or of public interest, or to prevent comment on matters in which the public has an interest or the right to be informed. Its underlying purpose being to protect privacy, in the case of a public figure—who by the very nature of being a public figure has no complete privacy—no liability exists when his or her name or picture is used without consent, or when the article complained of is of public interest, unless, of course, the publication is knowingly false (*Hemingway v. Random House, Inc.,* 23 N.Y. 2d 341, 296 N.Y.S. 2d 771, 244 N.E. 2d 250) or may be considered a blatant selfish,

commercial exploitation of the individual's personality. (*Gautier v. Pro-Football,* supra.) As stated by the Court of Appeals in *Spahn,* and quoted with approval by the United States Supreme Court in *Time, Inc. v. Hill,* 385 U.S. 374, 382, 87 S.Ct. 534, 17 L.Ed. 2d 456, "ever mindful that the written word or picture is involved, courts have engrafted exceptions and restrictions on to the statute to avoid any conflict with the free dissemination of thoughts, ideas, newsworthy events, and matters of public interest." . . .

It is quite apparent, therefore, that books and publications have a special position in the law. My distinguished colleague in dissenting puts it very aptly when he states that "[concededly book publishing, though a business, stands on a somewhat different plane than many other businesses in that freedom of the press is often involved]." Therefore, in considering books and publications, courts must take a broad view of what may or may not be written and what may or may not be said about books and their authors.

Under the *Rand* case, which was unanimously affirmed by the Court of Appeals of New York, we have another exception to the prohibition against the use of one's name or picture for advertising purposes without consent where book publishing is involved, under the principle that the right to discuss the work of a public figure in the literary world, to comment on it, or to criticize and compare it is within the public domain. We therefore find the courts "engrafting" exceptions and restrictions upon the right of privacy statute to avoid conflict with the free dissemination of thoughts, ideas, newsworthy events and matters of public interest.

In still another case, which clearly appeared to involve an advertising use of a picture without permission, the court interpreted the right of privacy statute so as to relieve the publisher of a newspaper of liability. The case is of interest not only to publishers but to advertisers, advertising agencies, and photographers as well. The magazine supplement of the New York *Herald Tribune* published two pictures of a girl model at the beach wearing what was called a "Poor-Boy Swim Suit." Some young boys were playing or standing in the vicinity of the model when she was photographed. The model was posed. Although the boys just happened to be nearby, they were clearly identifiable in the pictures.

The beach scene pictures were published with a note, including captions, purporting to be a fashion item, which indicated that the "Poor-Boy Swim Suit" was directly descended from a "big fad fashion" of the previous winter, the "Poor-Boy Sweater," which was launched by the French magazine *Elle*. The note ended with a statement that "the suit is by Elon, $20. Lord & Taylor."

Action was brought on behalf of several of the boys, who were less than ten years of age, under the right of privacy statute on the ground that their pictures were used for advertising without permission. The newspaper's motion to dismiss the complaint in advance of the trial was denied, and the newspaper appealed. The Appellate Division of the New York Supreme Court, in a 3 to 2 decision, reversed the lower court and dismissed the complaint (*Pagan v. New York Herald Tribune,* 32 A.D. 2d 341, 301 N.Y.S. 2d 120, June, 1969), holding that the use of the boys' pictures was not for advertising (although the accompanying fashion note referred to price and source where the item could be purchased) since they appeared only incidentally in the pictures. Consequently their use, in the light of the accompanying text, could be considered an item of legitimate public interest. The court said:

> Where a picture of an individual is published in a newspaper or magazine in connection with the presentation, without false or misleading material, of a matter of legitimate public interest to readers, and the picture bears a reasonable relationship to the presentation, the use of the picture in the publication is not actionable as a use for the purpose of advertising or trade within the prohibition of the statute unless the presentation is in effect an advertisement in disguise. . . .
>
> The decision in *La Forge v. Fairchild Publications,* supra, is sufficiently in point to be controlling. There, the defendant had published in its newspaper a two-page pictorial story entitled "Fashion Follows a Pattern." As noted in the memorandum of this court, the "spread" consisted of a dozen or more individual photographs taken at a racetrack of boys, young men and mature males each garbed in a sport jacket of a particular material. None of the individuals, including plaintiff, was identified by name or otherwise. The written matter accompanying the pictures stated, among other things, that the specified material of the jackets was a "runaway fashion at the races and associated events." This court concluded that the publication was not "for advertising purposes or for the purposes of trade" within the meaning of section 51 of the Civil Rights Law, citing *Dallesandro v. Henry Holt & Co.,* supra.

As mentioned above, this was a 3 to 2 decision. The dissenting judges felt that the case should not have been dismissed in advance of trial, because in their opinion there was an issue as to whether the picture and printed matter were "an advertisement in disguise."

ARTICLES OF FICTION

Nor is the use of photographs to illustrate articles of fiction too difficult an area. Some years ago a story appeared in a national magazine about a gunner on a Flying Fortress who was shot down during World War II. He had left a strange will, in which he bequeathed "one perfect rose" a week to a young lady who was a casual acquaintance. The magazine printed the picture of the young lady, as well as her name, and she sued for invasion of privacy. The court found that the story was not basically true, that the author had drawn somewhat upon a vivid imagination, and allowed recovery.[17]

In the following sections we shall see other examples of articles of public interest that by reason of inaccuracy, falsehood or distortion turn out to be fictional and consequently a use for purposes of profit or trade. We shall also see how the special rules affecting publishers of newspapers and magazines are applied in this area.

PURPOSES OF TRADE

In dealing particularly with classifications 3 and 4 of the Lahiri case (pictures used to illustrate items of news, immediate public interest, or of an educational or informative nature) the courts have found it necessary to explain that one cannot classify the use of a picture in a publication as being for "trade purposes" merely because a publisher seeks to make a profit from his magazine or newspaper.

In one sense every picture published in a newspaper or magazine is for the purpose of increasing circulation and increasing profits. In a photographic magazine, for example, the objective of the material is to teach and exhibit photographic excellence, and the pictures are selected for that reason even though the publisher profits by virtue of showing better pictures.[18]

In determining what is news or a matter of immediate public interest, the courts have assiduously avoided interpretations which could lead to encroachments upon freedom of the press. The courts have held, for example, that a scene in a newsreel of a group of women in a gymnasium attempting to reduce by means of various apparatus was a matter of public interest and not an invasion of privacy,[19] and ruled similarly where a passerby happened to get caught in a film of a crowd scene at an event of current interest.[20]

In this connection a decision of a federal court in a case brought against Dell Publishing Co. as a result of the publication in *Front Page Detective* of a picture which originally appeared in Pittsburgh newspapers back in 1953 is of interest.[21]

The plaintiffs in the case were the widow and children of a man who was kicked to death by hoodlums. In the January, 1954, issue of *Front Page Detective,* under the title of "Heartbreak House," there was a short account of the homicide and a picture. The suit was brought on a right of privacy theory and plaintiffs moved for summary judgment. The motion was denied by the U.S. District Court, and the Circuit Court affirmed. In arriving at its decision, the court said:

> But in this situation, the interest of the public in free dissemination of the truth and unimpeded access to news is so broad, so difficult to define and so dangerous to circumscribe that courts have been reluctant to make such factually accurate public disclosures tortious, except where the lack of any meritorious public interest in the disclosures is very clear and its offensiveness to ordinary sensibilities is equally clear.
>
> We concluded that the pictorially illustrated story of which plaintiffs complain is within the privilege which protects normal news items against claims of tortious invasion of privacy.

In a landmark case decided by the United States Supreme Court in January, 1967, 385 U.S. 374, the publishers of *Life* magazine were sued for falsely reporting that a new play portrayed an experience suffered by the Hill family. The article was entitled "True Crime Inspires Tense Play," with the subtitle "The ordeal of a family trapped by convicts gives Broadway a new thriller 'The Desperate Hours.' " The article then went on to show how a family rose to heroism in a crisis. *Life* magazine photographed the play, published some of the scenes, transported some of the actors to the house where the Hills had been held hostage, and re-enacted scenes from the play, which it also published. The pictures included shots of Hill's son being roughed up by one of the convicts, captioned "brutish convict," a picture of Hill's daughter biting the hand of a convict to make him drop a gun, captioned "daring daughter," and a picture of the father throwing his gun through the door after a "brave try" to save his family was foiled.

The facts were that the Hill family had been the subject of a front page story three years before as a result of having been held hostage for 19 hours by three escaped convicts in their suburban home in Whitemarsh, Pa. The family was released unharmed, and in an interview held with newsmen after the convicts departed, Mr. Hill stressed that the convicts had not molested them and had not been violent. The convicts were subsequently apprehended in an encounter with the police in which two of the convicts were killed. Thereafter, the Hill family moved to Connecticut and discouraged all efforts to keep them in the public spotlight through magazine stories or appearances on television.

The novel *The Desperate Hours* was published the year following the incident, but unlike the actual experience, the family in the story suffered violence at the hands of the convicts; the father and son were beaten, and the daughter subjected to verbal sexual insult. The book was then made into a play, *The Desperate Hours,* and *Life's* article concerning the play resulted in the lawsuit brought by the Hill family.

Life's defense was that the article was the subject of legitimate news interest and a subject of general interest and concern to the public at the time of publication and that it was published in good faith without any malice.

After the Hills won in the lower courts, *Life* appealed. The Appellate Courts affirmed the decision, and *Life* appealed to the United States Supreme Court, which heard argument on the case twice. Richard M. Nixon represented the Hills before the United States Supreme Court. However, notwithstanding the eminent counsel who later became our President, the Supreme Court set aside the judgment in favor of the Hills. The court said that the constitutional protection of free expression precludes the right of privacy action to redress false reports of newsworthy matters in the absence of proof that the publisher knew of such falsity or acted in reckless disregard of the truth. The court further ruled that erroneous statements about a matter of public interest, such as the opening of a new play linked to an actual incident, are inevitable and, if innocent or merely negligent, must be protected if freedoms of expression are to have the "breathing space" that they "need to survive." The court warned, however, that there is no constitutional protection of calculated falsehoods. Since the jury that had awarded $30,000 to the Hills after a second trial had not been properly instructed that such a verdict could only be predicated on a finding of knowing or reckless falsity in the publication of the article, the judgment was set aside and the case remanded for further proceedings.

The Supreme Court emphasized in the *Hill* case that a publication is not required to assume the impossible burden of verifying to a degree of certainty facts set forth in a news article associated with a person's picture or name and that liability will be imposed only where there is a calculated falsehood or reckless disregard for the truth:

> We create a grave risk of serious impairment of the indispensable service of a free press in a free society if we saddle the press with the impossible burden of verifying to a certainty the facts associated in news articles with a person's name, picture or portrait, particularly as related to non-defamatory matter. Even negligence would be a most elusive standard, especially when the content of the speech itself affords no warning of prospective harm to another through falsity. A negligence test would place on the press the intolerable burden of guessing how a jury might assess the reasonableness of steps taken by it to verify the accuracy of every reference to a name, picture or portrait.
>
> In this context, sanctions against either innocent or negligent misstatement would present a grave hazard of discouraging the press from exercising the constitutional guarantees. Those guarantees are

not for the benefit of the press so much as for the benefit of all of us. A broadly defined freedom of the press assures the maintenance of our political system and an open society. Fear of large verdicts in damage suits for innocent or merely negligent misstatement, even fear of the expense involved in their defense, must inevitably cause publishers to "steer . . . wider of the unlawful zone," *New York Times Co. v. Sullivan,* 376 U.S., at 279; see also *Speiser v. Randall,* 357 U.S. 513, 526; *Smith v. California,* 361 U.S. 147, 153-154; and thus "create the danger that the legitimate utterance will be penalized." *Speiser v. Randall,* supra, at 526.

But the constitutional guarantees can tolerate sanctions against *calculated* falsehood without significant impairment of their essential function. We held in *New York Times* that calculated falsehood enjoyed no immunity in the case of alleged defamation of a public official concerning his official conduct. Similarly, calculated falsehood should enjoy no immunity in the situation here presented us.

The *Hill* case is discussed under the heading of *purposes of trade* since one of the points raised by the Hills was that fictionalizing certain aspects of the story was done for purposes of trade; however, this case also fits under the headings of *fiction* and *public figures,* since the Hills did achieve wide publicity as a result of the experience where they were held as hostages.

Before leaving the heading *purposes of trade,* we might add a word about the display of pictures by a studio photographer. Under the New York right of privacy statute, the photographer may display pictures about his studio as samples of his work. This is not considered a use for trade purposes. If the subject objects, however, the photographer must remove the picture.

PUBLIC FIGURES

It has also been generally settled that public figures have little right of privacy. A statesman, actor, musician, or inventor who asks for and desires public recognition in a large sense surrenders his right of privacy to the public. When one obtains a photograph of such a person, and there is no breach of contract or confidence in the method in which it was obtained, he has the right to reproduce it, for informative purposes, whether in a newspaper, magazine or book.

One of the most interesting cases in this area involved the publication by the *New Yorker* magazine of a profile or biographical sketch in 1937. The plaintiff had been a child prodigy and had graduated from Harvard at the age of 16, at which time he received considerable publicity. The profile showed that the plaintiff had since become an eccentric recluse, and exposed in merciless fashion the failure of the plaintiff to live up to his early promise. Plaintiff sued for invasion of privacy and the court ruled for the defendant on the ground that plaintiff had been a public figure when a child, and that in 1937 there was still legitimate public interest in his career.[22]

The right of a public figure to privacy is clearly quite limited. One court said: "Persons who accept high positions ought not to be so tender about the mention of their names, they must bear 'the white light that beats upon a throne.' "[23]

On the other hand, the privilege of using the picture of a famous person as a subject of news or current interest or for informative purposes does not extend to the commercialization of his personality through forms of treatment distinct from dissemination of news or information.

In one case, a company had contracted with a number of baseball players to use, exclusively, the players' photographs in connection with the sale of the company's chewing gum. The defendant, a competing chewing gum company, used photographs of the same players in connection with the sale of its own chewing gum without plaintiff's consent. The first company brought an action against its competitor in the Federal courts and the court, in supporting the position of the plaintiff, pointed out that in addition to and independent of the right of privacy a man has a right in the publicity value of his photograph; that this right was particularly important to prominent persons and that far from having their feelings bruised through public exposure of their likenesses, they would feel sorely deprived if they no longer received money for authorizing advertisements and other commercial display of their likenesses. The court referred to this right as a "right of publicity." In effect, the court was pointing out that a baseball player's name and picture were valuable items and that he had a right to expect income from the commercial exploitation of his personality.[24]

In another case involving a famous baseball player (*Spahn v. Messner,* 18 N.Y. 2d 328, reargued 21 N.Y. 2d 124, appeal dismissed 393 U.S. 1046), Warren Spahn sought an injunction and damages against the unauthorized publication of what purported to be a biography of his life. The trial judge had found that "the record unequivocally establishes that the book publicizes areas of Warren Spahn's personal and private life albeit inaccurate and distorted and consists of a host, a preponderant percentage of factual errors, distortions and fanciful passages." The Court of Appeals of New York held that in these circumstances the publication was prohibited under the right of privacy statute and was not within the exceptions and restrictions for newsworthy events. The court made a clear distinction between Spahn's professional career, as to which no right of privacy exists, and the exploitation of his personality for commercial benefit, as to which his right of privacy clearly exists. The court said:

> But, it is erroneous to confuse privacy with "personality" or to assume that privacy, though lost for a certain time or in a certain context goes forever unprotected . . . . Thus it may be appropriate to say that the plaintiff here, Warren Spahn, is a public personality and that, insofar as his professional career is involved, he is substantially without a right to privacy. That is not to say, however, that his "personality" may be fictionalized and that, as fictionalized, it may be exploited for the defendants' commercial benefit through the medium of an unauthorized biography.

This portion of the opinion was quoted with approval by the United States Supreme Court in the *Hill* case discussed above.

The *Spahn* case, originally decided in October, 1966, was reargued in the Court of Appeals on remand by the United States Supreme Court, and on reconsideration the court adhered to its original decision in favor of Warren Spahn. The court's decision on the reconsideration, which came down in December, 1967, stated as follows:

The remand of this appeal by the Supreme Court gives us an opportunity to construe the statute so as to preserve its constitutionality . . . and to review the appeal in light of the standards set forth in *New York Times Co. v. Sullivan* (supra) and *Time, Inc. v. Hill.* . . .

[1] We hold in conformity with our policy of construing sections 50 and 51 so as to fully protect free speech, that, before recovery by a public figure may be had for an unauthorized presentation of his life, it must be shown in addition to the other requirements of the statute, that the presentation is infected with material and substantial falsification and that the work was published with knowledge of such falsification or with a reckless disregard for the truth.

[2] An examination of the undisputed findings of fact below as well as the defendants' own admission that "[i]n writing this biography, the author used the literary techniques of invented dialogue, imaginary incidents, and attributed thoughts and feelings" (brief for appellants, p. 10) clearly indicates that the test of *New York Times Co. v. Sullivan* (supra) and *Time, Inc. v. Hill* (supra) has been met here.

In another case decided by New York State's highest court, in December, 1968, (*Estate of Ernest Hemingway v. Random House Inc.,* 23 N.Y. 2d 341), the estate of this famous writer and his widow sought damages and an injunction against the author and publisher of a biography of Ernest Hemingway. Two of the grounds upon which the suit was based were that the author had wrongfully used material imparted in confidence and that the biography invaded the widow's right to privacy. The case was dismissed, and the dismissal upheld by the Appellate courts.

As to the right of privacy phase of the case, the Court of Appeals, in line with the *Spahn* and *Hill* cases ruled that a public figure—Mrs. Hemingway was held to be a public figure—may not bar the publication of an item of public interest in the absence of proof that the published matter was false and was published with knowledge of such falsity or in reckless disregard of the truth. The court said:

[13, 14] The fourth count—in which only Hemingway's widow asserts a cause of action—is grounded on the claim that the Hotchner book intrudes upon her privacy in violation of section 51 of the Civil Rights Law. The decisions in *Time, Inc. v. Hill,* 385 U.S. 374,

87 S.Ct. 534, supra, and *Spahn v. Julian Messner, Inc.,* 21 N.Y. 2d 124, 286 N.Y.S. 2d 832, 233 N.E. 2d 840, dispose of the point and confirm the correctness of the dismissal of this cause of action. Both of those cases establish that, in the light of constitutional guarantees of free speech, section 51 may not be applied to afford recovery to a public figure or in matters of public interest—to quote from *Hill,* 385 U.S. at p. 388, 87 S.Ct. at p. 542—"in the absence of proof that the defendant published the [item] with knowledge of its falsity or in reckless disregard of the truth." (See, also, *Spahn,* 21 N.Y. 2d . . . .) That Mrs. Hemingway is a public figure and newsworthy, within the meaning of these cases, may not be disputed. Not only is she the widow of a literary figure of world renown, a Nobel Laureate, but she herself has encouraged public attention to her status by writing articles for the popular magazines dealing with her husband and with events in their lives together. As the court aptly noted in *Goelet v. Confidential, Inc.,* 5 A.D. 2d 226, 228, 171 N.Y.S. 2d 223, 225, "[o]nce a person has sought publicity he cannot at his whim withdraw the events of his life from public scrutiny."

[15] With respect to the required proof of falsification, under the doctrine of the *Hill* and *Spahn* cases, we need but note that, despite a passing reference to the subject in an affidavit, no serious attempt was made to support such a claim. There was no allegation in the complaint of any misstatement knowingly or recklessly made, and in the proceedings below—as the court at Special Term, (MURPHY, J.) observed—counsel for the plaintiff appears to have "conceded" that no issue was presented as to the existence of "misstatements, inaccuracies or untruths." Our study of the papers before us confirms this conclusion.

In still another case decided since the last edition of our book (*Rosemont Enterprises Inc. v. Random House Inc. and John Keats,* 58 Misc. 2d 1, March, 1968), the New York Supreme Court decided that a biography of a public figure such as Howard Hughes falls within the constitutional protection for free speech and press and that no redress is available even for material and substantial falsification in the absence of proof that the book was published with knowledge of such falsity or in reckless disregard for the truth. The court further held that a public figure has no exclusive rights to his own life story and others need no consent or permission to write his biography. The court said:

[9, 10] The biography of Howard Hughes, published by defendants herein, irrespective of its literary merit or style . . . falls within those

"reports of newsworthy people or events" which are constitutionally protected and which are outside the proscription of the New York "Rights of Privacy" statute. The allegation that the book was published for "purposes of trade" and profit does not as plaintiff seeks to imply, alter its protected status. The publication of a newspaper, magazine, or book which imparts truthful news or other factual information to the public does not fall within "the purposes of trade" contemplated by the New York statute, even though such publication is published and sold for a profit. (See *Time, Inc. v. Hill* . . . .)

[11-13] The remaining ground on which plaintiff seeks to justify this suit is the assignment to it of Hughes' "right of publicity." This is a right that recognizes the pecuniary value which attaches to the names and pictures of public figures, particularly athletes and entertainers, and the right of such people to this financial benefit. It is not, however, every public use of a prominent person's name that he has a right to exploit financially. It is the unauthorized use in connection with the sale of a commodity for *advertising* purposes which is recognized as an actionable wrong under New York law. The same requirement of commercial use which limits the New York right of privacy inheres in the "right of publicity." (*Chaplin v. National Broadcasting Co.*, D.C., 15 F.R.D. 134; cf. *Haelan Laboratories v. Topps Chewing Gum*, 202 F. 2d 866.) The publication of a biography is clearly outside the ambit of the "commercial use" contemplated by the "right of publicity" and such right can have no application to the publication of factual material which is constitutionally protected. Just as a public figure's "right of privacy" must yield to the public interest so too must the "right of publicity" bow where such conflicts with the free dissemination of thoughts, ideas, newsworthy events, and matters of public interest.

[14] Because of such considerations, a public figure can have no exclusive rights to his own life story, and others need no consent or permission of the subject to write a biography of a celebrity. (See Hofstadter & Horowitz, *The Right of Privacy*, p. 59 . . . .)

In states which do not recognize the "right of publicity" as such,[25] the courts will often decide the same way on the same facts, speaking in terms of some limit to a public figure's waiver of his right of privacy. For example, in the case of *Bell v. Birmingham Broadcasting Co.*, 96 So. 2d 263 (Ala., 1957), the defendant broadcasting company caused an article to be published which included a photograph of announcer George Bell and the statement that Bell would announce all the University of Alabama football

games for defendant that season. The fact was that although Bell
and the broadcasting company had "opened negotiations" with
respect to having Bell announce the games, they had not concluded
a deal. Bell sued, charging that his name and picture had been used
for purposes of trade without his consent. The court held the article was really in the nature of an advertisement and that this was
an invasion of privacy. Although Bell, as a public figure, had re-
linquished part of his right of privacy, he was still entitled to be
protected from unauthorized commercial exploitation.

In a rather unusual case the television comedian Pat Paulsen,
who conducted a mock campaign for the Presidency in 1968, sued
to enjoin defendant from marketing a poster embodying his picture.
(*Paulsen v. Personality Posters Inc.,* N.Y. Supreme Court, 299
N.Y.S. 2d 501, October, 1968.) The poster was made up from an
unpublished photograph belonging to Pat Paulsen which had been
sent to defendant by his agent. The arrangement under which the
picture was sent to defendant was sharply in dispute. Paulsen
claimed that the picture was sent with an inquiry as to whether defendant would be interested in negotiating a license agreement with
royalties for its use. The defendant, on the other hand, claimed
that it was sent unsolicited with a request that it distribute the
picture in poster form to aid a publicity campaign on behalf of
Paulsen. The court denied Paulsen's application for a preliminary
injunction, holding that the right of privacy statute was not intended
to limit activities involving dissemination of news or information
concerning matters of public interest and that such activities are
privileged and do not fall within the scope of purposes of trade
even though they are carried on for a profit. The unusual part of
this case was that Paulsen claimed he was only kidding and his
presidential activities were just a publicity stunt. Nevertheless, this
was held to be a matter of public interest. The judge said:

> It is apparently plaintiff's position that since "he is only kidding"
> and his presidential activities are really only a "publicity stunt"
> they fall outside the scope of constitutionally protected matters of
> public interest. Such premise is wholly untenable. When a well-
> known entertainer enters the presidential ring, tongue in cheek or

otherwise, it is clearly newsworthy and of public interest. A poster which portrays plaintiff in that role, and reflects the spirit in which he approaches said role, is a form of public interest presentation to which protection must be extended. That the format may deviate from traditional patterns of political commentary, or that to some it may appear more entertaining than informing, would not alter its protected status. It is not for this or any court to pass value judgments predicated upon ephemeral subjective considerations which would serve to stifle free expression. "What is one man's amusement, teaches another's doctrine." (*Winters v. People of State of New York,* 333 U.S. 507, 510, 68 S.Ct. 665, 667, 92 L.Ed. 840.) Thus, whether the poster involved be considered as a significant satirical commentary upon the current presidential contest, or merely as a humorous presentation of a well-known entertainer's publicity gambit, or in any other light, be it social criticism or pure entertainment, it is sufficiently relevant to a matter of public interest to be a form of expression which is constitutionally protected and "deserving of substantial freedom."

Before leaving the subject of public figures, we note an item in *The New York Times* of May 31, 1970, to the effect that the Illinois Supreme Court has just upheld the dismissal of a $1.5 million suit by Nathan Leopold, who contended that his right to privacy was violated by the book *Compulsion* and the movie based on the book. Leopold, 65 years old, was paroled in 1963 after being imprisoned for the 1924 "thrill slaying" of Bobby Franks, age 14. Leopold's partner in the crime, Richard Loeb, was stabbed to death in prison in 1936.

The Illinois court said that the Constitution "assured liberty of expression in a matter of public interest and lasting public attention to the crime which became an American cause celebre."

INFORMATIVE AND EDUCATIONAL ARTICLES

The area of informative and educational articles (and the use of photographs to illustrate them) lies somewhere between current news and fiction. Here is how Justice Shientag described such articles in the Lahiri case:

They are not the responses to an event of peculiarly immediate interest, but, though based on fact, are used to satisfy an ever-present educational need. Such articles include, among others, travel stories, stories of distant places, tales of historic personages and events, the reproduction of items of past news and surveys of social conditions. These are articles educational and informative in character. As a general rule such cases are not within the purview of the statute.[27]

It is in this area that the courts appear to have the greatest difficulty striking a proper balance between the public interest in the dissemination of information and the preservation of an individual's privacy. One interesting case in New York, *Callas v. Whisper*,[28] involved the publication in a magazine of a photograph of plaintiff in a nightclub with a male companion. Plaintiff was merely a background figure in the photograph, which had been posed for the purpose of showing another person. The complaint alleged that plaintiff was an employee in the office of the publisher in a clerical capacity and that she had permitted defendants to take her picture upon the express understanding that they would not publish it. Plaintiff complained that the publication of her picture in a magazine which contained sensational and lurid articles gave the impression that she had been in a night club with a male companion and that she smoked and drank intoxicating beverages. The case was dismissed in advance of the trial, on the ground that it appeared from the plaintiff's own statement of her case in the court that the picture had not been used for advertising purposes or purposes of trade, and this decision was affirmed by the highest court in the State of New York.

In *Oma v. Hillman Periodicals, Inc.,* a 1953 New York case, *Pageant* magazine printed an article about the boxing profession. On the back cover appeared a photograph of plaintiff, identified by name, while the article made no mention of plaintiff whatsoever. The caption under the photograph referred the reader to the article inside. The court dismissed plaintiff's complaint based on violation of the Civil Rights Law, Sections 50 and 51, saying that this publication was not for the purposes of trade or advertising, but to illustrate an article of public interest. Explaining its conclusion further, the court noted that the illustration was relevant to the story, and that it is immaterial that it was also used to sell the article.

The case of *Dallesandro v. Henry Holt & Co.*, decided in 1957 by the Appellate Division in New York, involved a complaint under the New York Privacy Law, by a dock worker whose photograph appeared on the cover of a book entitled *Waterfront Priest*. The plaintiff was not identified by name on the cover or in the text of the book. The court, affirming dismissal of the complaint, stated:

> The book here involved purports to be the true story of a priest's "one-man crusade against gangsterism and terror on the New York Waterfront," and the book jacket showing the priest in earnest conversation with a longshoreman is an attempted pictorialization of the theme.
>
> It is immaterial that its manner of use and placement was designed to sell the articles so that it might be paid for and read (*Oma v. Hillman Periodicals, Inc.*, supra, 281. App. Div. at page 244, 118 N.Y.S. 2d at page 724).... The offending book jacket is annexed to the complaint, and since it appears therefrom that the use of the picture is not actionable under the civil rights law, the complaint was properly dismissed without leave to amend.

Yet in another cover-photograph case recently decided in New York (*Murray v. N.Y. Magazine Co.*, N.Y.L.J. 7/16/70), the Appellate Division of the Supreme Court in a 3 to 2 decision refused to grant the motion of the defendant magazine to dismiss without a trial the complaint of a person who was photographed on a public street wearing an Irish hat while watching the St. Patrick's Day parade. The picture appeared on the March 17, 1969, cover of the defendant's magazine without the plaintiff's consent. The magazine featured several articles, including one entitled "The Last of the Irish Immigrants." The dissenting judges held that since the photograph appeared in an issue that was published on St. Patrick's Day, it bore a reasonable connection to a matter of legitimate public interest, even though the picture had been taken two years before, and they cited the *Dallesandro v. Holt* case in support of their dissent. However, the majority of the court held that plaintiff is entitled to a trial on these facts. It is difficult to reconcile this case with the decision in the *Dallesandro* case, and it may be noted that the magazine has the right to appeal this case to the Court of Appeals. If such appeal is taken it will be interesting to see how New York's highest court rules on these facts.

We trust the cases described will at least show the photographer the broad outlines of the factors considered by the courts in this area.

THE DECENCY TEST

In most cases which have arisen outside of New York and the other statutory states listed previously, the courts have sought to determine whether a photograph would be offensive to the sensibilities of an ordinary person. In an action brought in the Federal courts some years ago,[29] Eleanor Sue Leverton, a minor, sued the Curtis Publishing Company for wrongful invasion of her right of privacy by publication of a photograph of her as she lay in the street immediately after being struck by an automobile. The photograph had originally appeared in a daily newspaper the day following the accident. Twenty months later it was used by the Curtis Publishing Company as an illustration for an article on traffic accidents, with emphasis on pedestrian carelessness, under the title "They Asked to be Killed." The court's decision for the plaintiff rested on two grounds:

(1) Even though the picture might not have lost its newsworthiness over a period of 20 months, the use of it to illustrate an article unrelated to the particular accident was not newsworthy and could, therefore, not be published under this exception to the rules governing invasion of the right of privacy.

(2) The question whether the publication of the photograph was offensive to ordinary sensibilities should be submitted to the jury.

In still another case, brought in California,[30] the publication of the photograph of a husband and wife in an affectionate position in a national magazine as part of an article on "Love" was held to be an invasion of privacy. Plaintiffs had been photographed while embracing and underneath the photograph appeared the caption, "Publicized as glamorous, desirable, 'Love at first sight' is a bad risk." Among other things, the court said that it was not unreasonable to believe the picture would be humiliating and disturbing to plaintiff's sensibilities, and that it could find no pertinency to the picture that would justify its use without consent. Note that the photograph in this case might, under some circumstances, be considered libelous because of its implications.

DISTINCTION BETWEEN DEFAMATION AND RIGHT OF PRIVACY

It is important for photographers to recognize the distinction between libel and the right of privacy. The two are often confused, but there are several differences which can be readily observed. First, libel is an injury to reputation — that is, injury in the eyes of others — while invasion of privacy involves an injury to one's own feelings — the right to be let alone.[31] In the case of the latter, it does not matter whether the publication has any effect on reputation. Second, truth is generally a defense in libel actions. Truth is no defense to an action for invasion of the right of privacy.

The United States Supreme Court in *New York Times Co. v. Sullivan,* 376 U.S. 254, formulated a guideline limiting the permissible scope of defamation actions by announcing "a federal rule that prohibits a *public official* from recovering damages for a defamatory falsehood relating to his official conduct unless he proves that the statement was made with 'actual malice'—that is, with knowledge that it was false or with reckless disregard of whether it was false or not." Next there occurred the extension of the *New York Times* rule to *public figures,* as we saw in the *Hill* and *Spahn* cases, which were right of privacy cases. The New York Supreme Court in a defamation case decided in November, 1969, (*Bavarian Motor v. Manchester,* 61 Misc. 2d 309) was called upon to rule on the sufficiency of a complaint in which the publisher of a nonfiction book on the history of the German Krupp family and its munitions works was charged with falsely stating that the German corporation went out of business and into oblivion. The publisher's motion to dismiss the complaint on the ground that it did not allege actual malice was denied. The court ruled that the plaintiff (the motor corporation) was not a *political or public figure* within the *New York Times* rule, which deprives a public official of legal redress for a defamatory falsehood without proof that the lie was a knowing one or was uttered in reckless disregard of the truth. The court noted that the rule had been extended to public figures in the *Hill* case, but refused to extend it further to include the plaintiff corporation, saying:

> Plaintiff herein, Bavarian Motor Works, appears not to be a public person within the purview of the *New York Times* line of cases. Further the defendants do not make even a colorable showing that it is such a person. Defendants' contention appears to be premised on the argument that the above-mentioned book is imbued with such public interest and furnishes so much information that it falls within the ambit of a "public issue" rationale and thereby deserves the "protection" of the *New York Times* rule. While the dissemination of historical information serves a most laudable educational need, it does not necessarily follow that by the mere fact of alleged libelous matter being contained therein, such matter is entitled to the benefit of the *New York Times* rule. To extend the *New York Times* rule to the circumstances herein would, it appears, be an unwarranted abridgment of private rights in the libel area and might very well be a further step to granting those in the position of the defendants a valid unconditional license, except where actual malice can be proved by the plaintiff. This court, mindful that such result might put at hazard those very rights and freedoms claimed by the defendants, is not about to so expand the *New York Times* rule.

We therefore see that notwithstanding the legal distinctions between defamation and right of privacy, the courts have granted to publishers constitutional protection of free speech and press in suits by public officials and public figures in both defamation and right of privacy cases. In the *Bavarian Motor* case, however, the court indicated that a state of flux prevails in this area of law. Future cases may interpret the law differently, and we caution our readers that competent legal advice should be obtained regarding any problem that a photographer or publisher may have in this area.

PRIVACY AND PROPERTY RIGHTS

The right of privacy belongs only to living persons. Deceased persons[32] (except in Utah by statute) and animals have no right of privacy,[33] nor do corporations, and the law is not applicable to pictures taken of private property. Yet the photographer's right to *use* the picture of an animal or private property may be challenged on other grounds, particularly where the use is for advertising purposes. (See the *Ylla* case in the next chapter on ownership of the photograph.[34]) In another interesting case, a famous photographer was sued for allowing the picture of an unusual tree which he had photographed to be used as calendar art and for other illustrative purposes. The theory of the complaint was that the owner of the tree had a property right which was being violated. The case was settled before it went to trial and the court thus did not have to decide the issue. Despite the fact that the plaintiff's theory in this case lacks the support of previous judicial determination, the photographer who wants to use pictures of private property for advertising illustrations should get a release if possible.

SUMMARY

Before turning to the subject of model releases, we should note once again that the right of privacy is not the same in all states and that in some states it has not even been recognized by the courts. It can be said that whether recognition of the right of privacy in a particular state is the result of a statute or judge-made law, the same decisions will generally be reached by the courts on similar sets of facts. At the same time, however, one cannot escape the fact that the states which have statutes similar to that of New York have construed the right of privacy more narrowly than those which do not. In some situations, therefore, jurisdictions not having a statute might reach a result favoring the plaintiff where a statutory state would not. These differences between the states — non-recognition of the right by some, statutory development in others, and non-statutory recognition in still others — make the model release a matter of paramount importance. When a photographer submits a photograph to a publisher, the publisher must be concerned with the law of all states where his magazine is sold, not just the law of the photographer's state.

The photographer might well ask where he stands in relation to the use made of pictures that he has sold to publications and that find their way into books and articles of the kind discussed in the various cases in this chapter. If the photographer knows that the pictures are to be used for advertising or trade purposes, he will be liable unless he has obtained a release from the subject. However, if the pictures are sold for editorial use, such as in a nonfiction book or in a magazine in connection with an article or item that is newsworthy or of general interest, it is unlikely that he would be liable if the pictures were misused, even though no release had been obtained. Nevertheless, we strongly suggest that the photographer's bill or invoice covering the sale of the picture state that it is being sold for editorial use only in order to protect the photographer who does not obtain a model release against a claim that he sold the picture with knowledge of its proposed improper use.

MODEL RELEASES

There can be no doubt that the photographer is well-advised to obtain model releases from his subjects whenever possible, even though at the time he takes the picture he may not expect to use it for a purpose proscribed by the laws concerning privacy. What kind of model release ("consent" is probably a better word since "model release" is merely the name used to describe the written instrument which embodies the consent of the subject) is required?

Under the New York statute the consent must be in writing. In states where the right of privacy is not statutory the consent may be oral. It is always much better, even where a written release is not required, to secure it in writing. It avoids the problem of proving oral consent in court or of asking the judge or jury to decide who is telling the truth as to whether the consent was obtained.

Although the New York statute requires written consent, oral consent may be pleaded as a partial defense in mitigation of damages, but not as a complete defense. For example, in the case of *Miller v. Madison Square Garden Corp.*,[35] a plaintiff had consented orally to the publication of his name and picture. It was also found that plaintiff had not been subjected to ridicule or humiliation as a result of the publication, and that he had suffered no damage. Under these circumstances the court awarded a verdict to the plaintiff for a technical violation of the New York statute: The sum of six cents for nominal damages.

Similarly, the oral consent of a parent was allowed as a partial defense in mitigation of damages where an action under the New York statute was brought by a minor.[36] In still another New York case where an actress sued for unauthorized use of her photograph for advertising purposes, it was held that defendant could plead as a partial defense the existence of a general custom in the theatrical profession under which persons in that profession permitted and encouraged the use of their pictures in advertisements without compensation and without their written consent.[37]

Must the photographer pay for a release for it to be effective? No. All that is required is the consent of the subject. Professional models who are paid for their services sign releases as a matter of course. An amateur who wishes to induce subjects to sign a release will usually be successful by the application of tact and the proffer of finished prints, and quite often tact alone will suffice.

While a model release is the photographer's best protection against right of privacy suits, it is not a guarantee that the photographer will not be sued. The broader the release, the greater the protection. Observe the language in releases A, B, C, D and E at the end of this chapter. They are all standard releases. Release A is the most comprehensive, but some photographers and advertising agencies prefer the simpler forms represented by B and C. Another form of release executed by the parent or guardian of a minor is shown in D. In E there is no reference to "valuable consideration" or "value received." As indicated above, payment is not necessary. Only consent is required, and some photographers may find it easier to get a subject's release if they use simpler language.

Even the comprehensive, detailed release will not prevent litigation in some situations. A good case in point is one in which a New York fashion model posed for an advertisement to promote a book club.[38] The picture showed her in bed reading a book. The model had signed a release for this picture. Subsequently the picture appeared in a different advertisement but it had been altered by changing the appearance of the man also in the picture. Underneath the photograph in the second advertisement was an invitation to readers to supply a caption to advertise bed sheets. The advertiser said that he tried to write such a caption but all he could come up with was "Lost Week-End," "Knight Errant," "Lost between the Covers," and "You can't go wrong with a Springmaid Sheet." The model sued for $50,000, charging she had not consented to the second use of the photograph and that she had been damaged socially and professionally by an ad which invited readers to make insinuations about her moral character. The advertiser countered that the model had signed a release which was sufficiently broad to allow the owner of the picture to use it as he saw fit.

The written release signed by the model expressly gave the photographer and "advertisers, customers, successors and assigns" the right to use the photograph for advertising and purposes of trade and "waived the right to inspect or approve the completed . . . pictures."

In denying the defendant's motion to dismiss the complaint, the court refused to accept any evidence that the model and the photographer had made an oral agreement that the picture was to be used *only* for the book club ad because of the existence of the signed release. Then the court said that although the release was sufficient to prevent the model from recovering damages for re-use of the picture in its original form, it was not at all clear that it included permission to alter the picture and then republish it, since the waiver of the right to inspect or approve the picture applied only to the photographer's original finished product. This case never reached trial, and so there was no final decision as to whether or not the release did, in fact, cover the second advertisement. The decision on the motion to dismiss the complaint, however, demonstrates how the question of the scope of a consent may be raised and once again illustrates the dangers of altering or retouching a photograph. In such cases the model may well ask a question which the court posed in this decision — is this the photograph for which she granted a consent?

In still another case,[39] where the release contained a statement that the picture could be used "in whole or in part," or "composite or distorted" in character or form, and where the model waived the right to inspect or approve the picture before its use, the model brought suit to recover damages for libel, claiming that the photograph had been published depicting her without her hair in an advertisement bearing the caption, "All Bald-up on Hair-dos?"

The lower court ruled that even though the release stated that there could be a distorted representation, this did not permit a use which would hold the subject up to ridicule and hence be libelous. The publisher appealed this decision and the Appellate Court ruled that it could not be determined from the release exactly what the publisher could do under the clause of the release permitting use of the picture in composite or distorted form. The court said it may very well be that the parties intended that defendant might do exactly what was complained of by the model and that the publisher should not be denied the right to prove that fact. Thus, if the release itself is clear as to what liberties may be taken with the picture, it may well be that the model cannot later be heard to complain.

Note that this case is different from the Burton case which involved an ad for Camel cigarettes and which we will discuss at the beginning of the chapter on libel, Chapter 7. In the "Hair-Do" case the release specifically covered the question of distortion. From the standpoint of the photographer, then, it is best to use the detailed release covering such matters as blurring, distortion, alterations and others (Model Release Form A).

MODEL RELEASE FORM A

In consideration of my engagement as model, upon the terms hereinafter stated, I hereby give X, his legal representatives and assigns, those for whom X is acting, and those acting with his authority or permission, the absolute right and permission to copyright and/or use, re-use and/or publish, and/or republish photographic portraits or pictures of me or in which I may be included, in whole or in part, or composite or distorted in character or form, without restriction as to changes or alterations from time to time, in conjunction with my own or a fictitious name, or reproductions thereof in color or otherwise made through any media at his studios or elsewhere for art, advertising, trade, or any other purpose whatsoever.

I also consent to the use of any printed matter in conjunction therewith.

I hereby waive any right that I may have to inspect and/or approve the finished product or products or the advertising copy or printed matter that may be used in connection therewith or the use to which it may be applied.

I hereby release, discharge, and agree to save harmless X, his legal representatives or assigns, and all persons acting under his permission or authority or those for whom he is acting, from any liability by virtue of any blurring, distortion, alteration, optical illusion, or use in composite form, whether intentional or otherwise, that may occur or be produced in the taking of said picture or in any subsequent processing thereof, as well as any publication thereof even though it may subject me to ridicule, scandal, reproach, scorn and indignity.

I hereby warrant that I am of full age and have every right to contract in my own name in the above regard. I state further that I have read the above authorization, release and agreement, prior to its execution, and that I am fully familiar with the contents thereof.

Date ....

Name .... (L.S.)

Witness ....

Address ....

MODEL RELEASE FORM B

For good and valuable consideration, the receipt of which is hereby acknowledged, I hereby consent that the photographs of me taken by John Doe, proofs of which are hereto attached, or any reproduction of the same, may be used by John Doe or his assigns or licensees for the purpose of illustration, advertising, trade, or publication in any manner.

Signed ....

Address ....

Date ....

MODEL RELEASE FORM C

I, (we) .... being of legal age hereby consent and authorize (client name), its successors, legal representatives and assigns, and the ABC Agency, Inc., ..., New York, N. Y., its successors, legal representatives and assigns, to use and reproduce my name and photograph (or photographs) taken by .... on (date) and circulate the same for any and all purposes, including publication and advertising of every description. Receipt of full consideration of $................................

is here acknowledged and no further claim of any kind will be made by me. No representations have been made to me.

....
(Name)

....
(Address)

MODEL RELEASE FORM D

I hereby affirm that I am the parent (guardian) of (name) and for value received and without further consideration I hereby irrevocably consent that each of the photographs which have been taken of him (her) by (name of photographer) and/or his (her) assigns may be used for advertising, trade, illustration, or publication in any manner.

....
(Name of parent or guardian)

....
(date)

MODEL RELEASE FORM E

Date ....

Place ....

I hereby consent to the use by you, or by anyone you authorize, for the purpose of advertising or trade, of my name and/or a portrait, picture or photograph of me, or any reproduction of same in any form.

Name ....

The language of form D may be added to A, B, C or E when a minor is involved.

REVIEW

A recapitulation of a few of the rules concerning model releases may be helpful.

(1) Although the written consent is not necessary in many states, it is sound practice to get the release in writing.

(2) The consent of a minor to use a picture is not adequate. The release should be signed by the parent or guardian. It isn't always safe to accept an unsupported statement that a young person is over 21.

(3) The use made of a picture must not go beyond the limits set forth in the release.

(4) The release must be voluntary. If secured by fraud, the consent is not effective.

Finally, it should be remembered that what we have said here with respect to the right of privacy is not intended as an exhaustive analysis of the subject. The right of privacy is a relatively new area of law. Interpretations of the law may vary from state to state and as conditions change, so will the law of privacy. Nevertheless, we are confident that photographers will find proper guidance in the rules which we have set forth here.

NEW YORK RIGHT OF PRIVACY STATUTE

§50 Right of Privacy

A person, firm or corporation that uses for advertising purposes, or for the purposes of trade, the name, portrait or picture of any living person without having first obtained the written consent of such person, or if a minor of his or her parent or guardian, is guilty of a misdemeanor.

§51 Action for Injunction and for Damages

Any person whose name, portrait or picture is used within this state for advertising purposes or for the purposes of trade without the written consent first obtained as above provided may maintain an equitable action in the supreme court of this state against the person, firm or corporation so using his name, portrait or picture to prevent and restrain the use thereof; and may also sue and recover damages for any injuries sustained by reason of such use and if the defendant shall have knowingly used such person's name, portrait or picture in such manner as is forbidden or declared to be unlawful by the last section, the jury, in its discretion, may award exemplary damages. But nothing contained in this act shall be so construed as to prevent any person, firm or corporation, practicing the profession of photography, from exhibiting in or about his or its establishment specimens of the work of such establishment, unless the same is continued by such person, firm or corporation after written notice objecting thereto has been given by the person portrayed; and nothing contained in this act shall be so construed as to prevent any person, firm or corporation from using the name, portrait or picture of any manufacturer or dealer in connection with the goods, wares and merchandise manufactured, produced or dealt in by him which he has sold or disposed of with such name, portrait or picture used in connection therewith; or from using the name, portrait or picture of any author, composer or artist in connection with his literary, musical or artistic productions which he has sold or disposed of with such name, portrait or picture used in connection therewith. As amended L. 1911, c. 226; L. 1921, c. 501, eff. May 3, 1921.

CHAPTER III

Who Owns The Picture?

ONE OF THE EARLIEST principles established by a court in the area of photography was that the relationship between a photographer and his (paying) customer is that of employer and employee. In 1913 a New York court ruled:

> It is settled law that the ordinary contract between a photographer and his customer is a contract of employment. The conception as well as the production of the photograph is work done for the customers, and they, not their employee, are the exclusive owners of all proprietary rights.[1]

It is the law today that in the absence of an agreement to the contrary, in the usual customer-photographer relationship, ownership of the picture is vested in the customer.

Although the rule that a paying customer owns the photograph was established many years ago, it was less than 25 years ago that the question as to who retains the negative came directly before the courts for the first time. Two cases arose in New York on this point.

In the first case,[2] decided in 1946, a court found that there had been an agreement between the photographer and his customer under which the negatives as well as the prints were to be delivered to the customer. The judge who decided the case also went so far as to say that even without an agreement, the negatives belonged to the customer, holding that by virtue of the relationship between the photographer and the customer a contract is implied in law whereby the customer retains all proprietary rights in the pictures and negatives.

In 1947 a case arose from a situation in which no agreement had been made as to who would keep the negatives.[3] In that case the defendant, a professional photographer, was hired to make photographs of plaintiff and several others. The order was in writing and included such items as the number of prints and the price. However, nothing was said regarding the negatives. After the pictures were delivered the customer asked for the negatives and upon the photographer's refusal to deliver them, commenced suit. The customer won in the lower court, but on appeal the decision was reversed and the photographer was held entitled to retain the negatives. Evidence was introduced in this case that there has always been an established custom in the field that negatives are kept by the photographer. Since there was no agreement as to the negatives, the Appellate Court said that the custom in the field should govern.

However, it must be made clear at this point that although the photographer has the right to *retain* the negatives in the absence of an agreement to the contrary, he has no right to *use* them. Note the language of the court on that point:

> It is true that the photographer's right to retain the negatives gives him no right to use them for any purpose whatsoever, except at the request of the customer. The photographer cannot sell the negatives nor make photographs from them for anyone except the customer ...
> There is nothing inconsistent with proprietary rights in the customer and the holding that the custody of the plates should remain with the photographer. This view would seem to represent the expectation of the parties in the absence of any special agreement to the contrary ...
> We hold, therefore, that where a customer employs a photographer to make pictures of him, the photographer, in the absence of an agreement to the contrary, has the right to retain the negatives. He may not, however, make any use of the negative without the permission of the customer.

The above case was decided by three judges. The excerpt from the opinion set forth represents the views of two of the judges. The third judge went even further. He based his decision not only on the custom of the trade but said that the photographer has not only the right to custody of the negative but is the actual owner of the negative. His opinion says:

> In my opinion a photographer owning a plate or film which, upon employment, is furnished as part of the transaction of taking a photo-

graph for a customer, continues in such ownership in the absence of agreement providing otherwise. As in the process of photography the designated object is produced as an image on such plate or film the photographer's ownership is subjected to a limitation by which the negative may only be used for such reproduction as the customer authorizes. Difference of such limitation in respect of private and public persons is not involved or considered.

This may be a significant decision for photographers, even though it represents the opinion of just one court in the State of New York, since the right to retain a negative could provide a measure of control not attainable when both ownership of the picture and custody of the negative are in the customer. There are still too many unanswered questions, however, for one to speak with assurance on this point, and it is possible that the advances in reproduction of photographs directly from prints and transparencies may make the entire question of custody of the negative moot.

Another interesting case on ownership of photographs was decided by a Federal court in New York in 1956.[4] The plaintiff, a commercial photographer, was retained by an advertising agency to take a picture for use in a specific advertisement. The photographer delivered the negative to the agency at its request, and the agency proceeded to sell the picture to another advertiser without the photographer's consent. The photographer sued the agency for infringement of copyright, claiming that he was the beneficial owner of the picture, because under existing trade usage there was an implied agreement that the photographer retained ownership of the picture. The court held that evidence of trade usage was inadmissible to contravene the "general rule of law" which vests ownership of a delivered photograph in the customer rather than the photographer.

It would appear that the court's decision was based on the assumption that the relationship between a commercial photographer and an advertising agency is not distinguishable from that between a portrait photographer and his customer.[5]

Under rules generally followed by the courts today, where a photographer receives an assignment from a magazine to take certain pictures for a fee, ownership of the photograph will be in the magazine, unless a contract provides otherwise.

What has been said about the ownership of pictures and negatives where there is an agreement for payment has no application
to a case where the photographer acts on his own initiative in taking
the pictures.

In a case in 1894,[6] the photographer took a picture of a
famous actress and had the picture copyrighted. The picture was
published in a newspaper without the consent of the photographer
and he instituted suit for infringement. The court held that where
the photographer takes the picture on his own he is the author and
proprietor of the photo and negatives. The court said:

> But when a person submits himself or herself as a public character,
> to a photographer, for the taking of a negative, and the making of
> photographs therefrom for the photographer, the negative, and the
> right to make photographs from it, belong to him. He is the author
> and proprietor of the photograph, and may perfect the exclusive
> right to make copies by copyright.

The court concluded that the photo had not been made for
the actress who sat for it and that she was not the customer. The
fact that she was the subject of the picture did not make it hers.
The court held that the picture belonged to the person for whom
it was made and since it was made for the photographer, he and
he alone owned the picture and negative. This is still the law today.

There are fringe situations in which an element of compensation to the photographer may be involved without giving rise to the
relationship of photographer and customer. For example, where
high school students hired a photographer to make a class picture
without paying him for taking the photo but with the understanding
that he could sell the pictures individually to students, it was decided the proprietary rights in the picture and the negative belonged
to the photographer and that he could obtain the copyright.[7]

Another interesting situation occurred in a case decided in
the New York courts in 1957.[8] A photographer who specialized in
taking portraits of famous people arranged for an exhibit of portraits of prominent architects and sculptors. The photographer requested a well-known architect to pose for a picture to be used in
·this exhibition, and asked him to contribute $25 towards the cost
of the exhibit, which the architect paid. The photographer then

placed a copyright notice on the picture and used it in the exhibition. Subsequently the photographer filed a copy of the picture with the Copyright Office.

Several years later the architect purchased several prints from the photographer and turned over one of the prints to a magazine which used it in an advertisement for a commercial concern. This was done with the express consent of the architect but without the knowledge or consent of the photographer. The photographer sued in a New York State court to recover damages for the unauthorized use of the picture. A $200 award to the photographer was reversed by the higher court on the ground that since a copyright was involved the state courts had no jurisdiction; the photographer was told by the court that he would have to sue in Federal court for copyright infringement.

One aspect of this case, however, is worthy of mention in this chapter. The question was presented as to whether the payment of the $25.00 by the subject to defray the expense of the exhibit gave the subject the proprietary rights in the picture or whether such rights remained with the photographer. On this point the lower court ruled squarely in favor of the photographer, saying:

> In the instant case the plaintiff (the photographer) requested Reinhardt (the architect) to sit for her in connection with her exhibition; the photograph was to be used for plaintiff's benefit. While . . . (the architect) paid her $25 at that time such payment was made not for the portrait, but in order to defray costs of plaintiff's exhibit. Under these circumstances, an implied contract must be said to have existed between . . . (them) pursuant to which all proprietary interest in Reinhardt's photograph, including the right of copyrighting the same, would lie solely with the plaintiff, and not with Reinhardt.

Since this point was not involved in the appeal, which centered solely around the copyright phase, we regard the ruling as to the effect of the token payment to be an indication that courts will not divest photographers of proprietary rights in their pictures merely because some payment was made, but will inquire into the purpose of the payment. This is especially so where the photographer claims that a true relationship of photographer and customer did not exist.

In another case[9] the late Ylla, famous photographer of animals, was sued by the owner of a dog. The owner requested Ylla to make pictures of her dog with the understanding that she would select and pay for those prints which she wanted. Subsequently, Ylla's agent sold one of the pictures to a commercial concern for advertising purposes and the picture appeared in newspapers.

While one of the points in this case involved the New York right of privacy statute (which is treated elsewhere in this book) and the court held that the right of privacy statute had no application to animals, the question of proprietary rights in the pictures was also in issue. The court said:

> If, for example, a photograph of a dog happens to be taken by a photographer on his own initiative without any arrangement with the owner of the dog, the owner making no payment therefor, all proprietary interest in that photograph, including the right to copyright the same, lies solely with the photographer (*Altman v. New Haven Union Co.*, 254 F. 113). On the other hand, as in this case, if the photograph is taken at the request of the owner of the animal who pays the photographer for making it, all proprietary interest in that photograph, including the right to copyright it, lies with the owner (*Press Pub. Co. v. Falk*, 59 F. 324; *Holmes v. Underwood & Underwood, Inc.*, 225 App. Div., 360, Supra).[10]

The court then granted an injunction to the owner of the dog restraining the photographer, the advertising agency and advertiser from any further use of the dog's picture.

It is important to remember, as we have shown, that, depending on the circumstances, the ownership of the prints, the ownership of the negative, the right to possession of the negative, and the right to reproduce the picture can all be separate and distinct, and can be divided differently between the photographer and his customer and/or subject, and others. For further discussion of the right to reproduce the picture, see *Chapter 6, infra*, on *Copyrights*.

CHAPTER IV

Loss Of and Damage To Film

DURING PROCESSING

As noted in the original edition of this book, there was a dearth of legal precedent on the subject until May 15, 1962, when the Appellate Division in New York decided the case of *Willard Van Dyke Productions, Inc. v. Eastman Kodak Company*.[1] The case was appealed again and in 1963 the intermediate appellate decision was affirmed by New York's highest court, the Court of Appeals.[2]

Now for the first time we have a clear and definite expression of judicial opinion from the highest court of a state on the legal effect of the legend which has appeared for many years on the packaged film of Eastman Kodak Company.

In this case, the plaintiff, Willard Van Dyke Productions, Inc., had purchased a quantity of Kodak Ektachrome Commercial 16mm film. Each of the rolls of film was packaged in a container upon which appeared the words "Film Price Does Not Include Processing" and, in much smaller type, the following notice:

"Read This Notice"

"This film will be replaced if defective in manufacture, labeling, or packaging, or if damaged or lost by us or any subsidiary company. Except for such replacement, the sale or subsequent handling of this film for any purpose is without warranty or other liability of any kind. Since dyes used with color films, like other dyes, may, in time, change, this film will not be replaced for, or otherwise warranted against, any change in color."

The particular film was purchased by the photographer to be used in fulfilling a contract with a third party for photographing certain facilities in Alaska. After purchasing the film, the photographer took it to Alaska and shot his pictures. It was conceded that the film was properly exposed and that if correctly developed would have resulted in a negative from which commercially valuable prints could be made and which could have been fully satisfactory to fulfill the photographer's contract with the third party.

After exposing the films, the photographer returned the film to New York, where it was forwarded to Eastman Kodak's laboratory for processing. It was conceded that the film was in good condition when received by Eastman Kodak, but during the development a substantial portion of the film was damaged by a deposit of foreign material and by rub marks in such a way that it became commercially valueless. It was further conceded that the damage was not intentional or malicious but, of course, negligence was not ruled out.

The photographer then had to return to Alaska and retake the shots which had been ruined in processing and brought suit for $1,537.50 to cover rephotographing the necessary sequences.

It appears that in accordance with the terms of the legend, Eastman Kodak had reimbursed the photographer for the cost of the film plus processing and claimed that it was under no further liability. This claim was immediately rejected by the Court on the basis that there was no proof that the photographer had accepted the same in full settlement of the claim. The Court held that such payment was merely for a portion of the photographer's claim which was conceded to be owing and would not bar the photographer from recovering for the additional items of damage which were in dispute.

Coming to the important legal points of the case which are of interest to all photographers and processors alike, the Court held that there were two separate transactions here, (1) the purchase of the film and (2) the processing, and since the legend on the package of film expressly stated that the cost of the film did not include processing, the attempt of Eastman Kodak to limit its liability for processing to the cost of replacement of the film and cost of processing necessarily failed and Eastman Kodak had to answer to the photographer in damages, which in this case amounted to $1,537.50.

The Appellate Division said:

There were two separate transactions. First, there was a sale of film by the defendant to plaintiff. In connection with such transaction the plaintiff was given express notice by the defendant that the price paid by plaintiff for the film did not include processing. Thus, the matter of the processing was left for future bargaining. Then, it was some time after the completion of the sale that the defendant received the exposed film from plaintiff and undertook the development thereof. This other transaction, separate and distinct from the original sales contract, was in the nature of a bailment for mutual benefit . . .

There was no written or formal contract entered into between the parties for the development of the exposed film. The film was delivered to and accepted by the defendant for processing work thereon without the statement then of any conditions. Thus, there being no agreement to the contrary, the defendant, on undertaking this work, was obliged to perform it with ordinary care and skill.

The Court then noted that Eastman Kodak did not claim that it was under no obligation to use care and skill, saying:

The defendant does not claim it was not so bound. It is not the defendant's contention that there was an agreement exempting it from the duty to exercise due care. Even the terms of the notice upon the label accompanying the sale of film are not claimed by defendant to have the effect of relieving it from such duty. Defendant's position is merely that, by virtue of the terms of the notice, there was an agreement limiting its liability for any damage to the film to the replacement thereof whether or not such damage was occasioned by reason of its alleged negligence.

The Court was careful to point out that a valid agreement could have been made limiting the liability for processing to replacement of the film but that such an agreement did not exist under the facts of this case where the cost of the film did not include processing and no separate agreement was made as to the processing which included a limitation of liability.

We now quote the opinion written by the Court of Appeals in affirming the decision rendered by the Appellate Division:

> The law looks with disfavor upon attempts of a party to avoid liability for his own fault and, although it is permissible in many cases to contract one's self out of liability for negligence, the courts insist that it must be absolutely clear that such was the understanding of the parties. In other words, it must be plainly and precisely provided that "limitation of liability extends to negligence or other fault of the party attempting to shed his ordinary responsibility." . . . In line with this principle, we have consistently decided that contracts will not be construed to absolve a party from, or indemnify him against, his own negligence, unless such intention is expressed in unequivocal terms.

The Court of Appeals then concluded, and this may be regarded as the holding of the case, that where the limitation of liability is on the package of film and the price of the film does not include processing, the limitation is not binding on the photographer whose film is ruined in processing. In other words, the previous limitation at the time of the purchase of the film applied to that purchase only and did not carry over into the separate processing transaction, even though the same company was involved and it had spoken in terms of "any subsequent handling" at the time of the purchase. In the absence of clear proof that the limitation of liability was agreed upon as part of the processing contract, the photographer was not barred from recovering the full amount of damages suffered as a result of the ruining of his film.

While this case has gone a long way to clarify the uncertainty previously existing as to the effect of this legend on packaged film where the cost of the film does not include processing, the question is still open as to the effect of such a legend where the cost of the film includes processing and it can be shown that such a covenant of limitation of liability was a factor influencing the bargain for the processing.

Perhaps a case will arise where this specific question will be presented to an appellate court for decision. However, the language of the Court in the above case indicated quite clearly that the limitation of liability must not only be clearly expressed but the processor must also show that the film was delivered for processing with complete understanding of such limitation. The Appellate Division said on this point:

> Consequently, a bailee (which is what the person receiving film for processing would be) relying upon an agreement to cut down the full measure of its common-law responsibility for negligence is bound to show that the bailor (the photographer) with complete understanding that such was to be the agreement, gave assent thereto. (Matter in parenthesis represents comment of authors.)

Most camera stores and other processors give the photographer a receipt for the film when it is delivered for developing. These receipts invariably contain a legend limiting the processor's liability for loss or damage to the cost of replacement of the film. The photographer rarely reads the terms of the receipt unless the film is lost or damaged and then for the first time he becomes aware of the limitation of liability. Normally a person who signs a contract without reading it is still bound by its terms. However, a receipt is not signed by the photographer and a receipt is not a contract. Therefore we get back to the all-important question of whether the photographer was aware of the limitation of liability at the time he delivered or sent the film in for processing.

If the processor can show that the photographer was given notice of the limitation of liability — even if he didn't expressly agree to such limitation — the photographer might be considered to have implicitly agreed by leaving his film under such conditions, and would therefore be bound by the limitation. However, this is most difficult to prove and since the law does not look with favor upon such agreements, the burden of proof would be on the processor. There is, however, one reported case decided by a court in New York where the limitation of liability in the receipt was held binding on the photographer. The Court reasoned that if the photographer didn't read the receipt at the time he brought the film in for processing, it was his own fault. However, this was a decision of a lower court in 1941. In view of the decision of the Court of Appeals in the Eastman Kodak case in 1963, we believe (in the absence of clear proof that the photographer had notice of or agreed to the limitation of liability on the receipt) that the photographer's claim for damages would not be defeated by the usual small-print limitation of liability.

There is an unreported case in 1951 in which one of the authors successfully represented a photographer in similar circumstances.[4] The photographer had been engaged to take pictures of a high school girl going to her first prom. He was to receive a fixed sum for the pictures. After taking them, he brought the film to a camera store for processing. He had previously made several test shots with the same film to make certain that there was nothing wrong with the film. The exposed film was ruined in processing and the photographer sued to recover the full price he would have received from his client less the expenses of the film and processing. The camera shop's defense was that the processing was done by a third party and that the receipt contained a clause limiting its liability to the cost of replacement of the film. The photographer countered by proving that he had been doing business with the camera shop for a long time; was well known to its employees; that they often didn't bother to give him a receipt; that no receipt was issued on this occasion; and that when he called for the pictures they gave them to him without even asking for a receipt. The Court accepted the photographer's version of the facts and awarded him judgment of the full amount claimed. Unfortunately, the Court did not write any legal opinion which might serve as a precedent for later cases.

One further point should be noted before leaving this subject.

The Courts have repeatedly held that such a limitation of liability must be strictly construed against the party who prepares the receipt. In the Eastman Kodak case, the Appellate Division said:

> The terms must be strictly construed . . . and most strongly against the defendant, it being defendant's draftmanship paring down the ordinary rights of its customers . . .
>
> Inasmuch as the parties were then contracting with reference to the sale of film, with processing expressly excluded, the statements in the notice, strictly construed, are referrable only to the warranties and liabilities in connection with the sale of the unexposed film. The provision for the limitation of defendant's liability in connection with the subsequent handling of the film for any purpose; would be confined to a limitation of liability in the subsequent handling of the

unexposed film for any purpose in connection with the sale. More-over the word "handling" used in connection with the unexposed film, narrowly construed, would not include processing, involving as it does, more than the mere handling of such film, namely, special-ized work on exposed film with the use of materials and technical equipment. If the defendant had intended to broaden the scope of the limiting provisions to embrace liability in connection with such work, we may infer that it would have used the words "develop-ment" or "processing" which are terms readily understood in the field of photography.

This means that unless the terms of the limitation of liability are clear that it is intended to cover the type of claim involved, the question of whether or not the photographer had notice of the terms could be immaterial. For example, if the limitation of liability in the receipt covers damage in processing, it will not be deemed to include a claim for loss of film in processing.

It can therefore be readily seen that many complex legal questions enter into the field of the photographer-processor relationship and that, in the final analysis, the answer depends on the facts in each particular case except for situations which clearly fall within the pattern of the cases discussed in this chapter.

UNDEVELOPED FILM LOST IN TRANSIT

In a decision handed down by the New York Supreme Court in 1950[5] and upheld on appeal by the Appellate Division, a professional photographer recovered over $4,000 in a judgment against Railway Express Agency for the loss of exposed but undeveloped film. Forty-three sheets of color film contained in a package were delivered to Railway Express for shipment to Eastman Kodak Company. They were lost en route. The photographer insured the film for $5,000 and paid the required premium. The exposures were made of scenes which the photographer took during a long trip through the western part of the United States for that express purpose. He was a free lance photographer and the scenes were shot for sale to prospective customers, mainly calendar manufacturers.

The case was unusual in that there were no legal precedents. Railway Express claimed that even though the film was insured for

No risk is involved and no consent is necessary when persons appearing in a picture are unrecognizable. But remember that a person may be identifiable even though you do not show his face in the picture.

This appealing photograph looks safe, but it was used in an advertisement and the photographer had to produce a release signed by the parents of the child.

Photographs used as illustrations in this book are copyrighted by Ziff-Davis Publishing Co. and are used by permission of Popular Photography magazine.

Public figures, such as Jimmy Durante, get less protection under privacy law, but their pictures may not be used in an ad without their consent.

It is generally stated that photographs of houses or other property may be published without obtaining the consent of the owner, since ordinarily only living persons have a right of privacy. But owners of property might bring suit on other legal grounds.

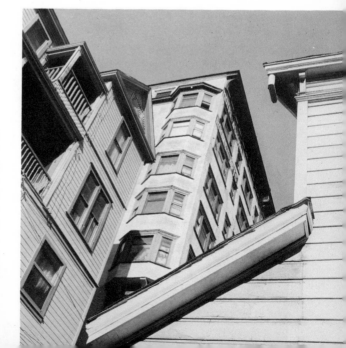

No one could take offense at the picture of this infant, but the photographer should bear in mind that the use of the picture in most states for advertising or trade purposes will be an invasion of privacy.

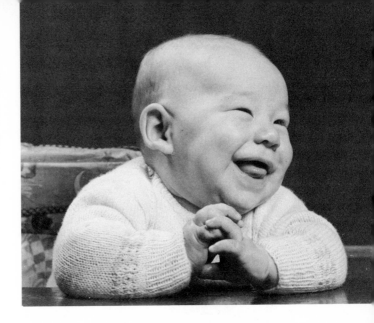

Candid shots of people like this one are among the most popular type of pictures made by amateurs today. Generally, when used for editorial purposes, they require no model releases. Yet because of the way in which such pictures are taken, often unknown to the subject, they can be a potent cause of privacy lawsuits.

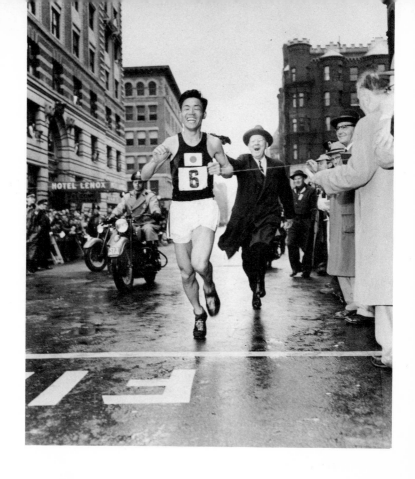

News pictures used to report current events or items of public interest may be published without obtaining the consent of the persons in them.

$5,000, the plaintiff's recovery must be limited to the actual value of the film, and that unless the plaintiff could prove that the undeveloped film had a value, all they had to pay was the purchase cost of new film.

However, the photographer was able to prove all the necessary elements of his case. He proved that he had previously made test shots from film with the same emulsion number which had been processed satisfactorily. He proved that he had used due care and skill in taking the pictures. He subpoenaed the records of Eastman Kodak Company, showing that previous processing done for him over a period of four years had been satisfactory and that the quantity of defective film was infinitesimal. Market value of the lost film was established through records of the photographer showing prior sales of similar pictures.

This case preceded the Willard Van Dyke case in recognizing that the value of film comes into existence the moment the photographer takes his shot, and not when the film is later successfully developed. It was the first case we know of where a substantial value was fixed by a court on undeveloped film. The actual decision of the court was very brief, however, and did not discuss the fine legal points involved.

Here again it must be noted that the relationship between the owner of the film (the bailor) and the carrier (like the processor, a bailee) is fixed by contract. The sender is requested to declare a value on the shipment. Naturally, if you declare a value of $50, that is the most you will get if there is a loss in transit. Therefore, the photographer must be careful when sending his film anywhere to make sure that a proper value is placed on it. It costs a little extra for the added value, but will be well worth it in the event of loss.

FINISHED PICTURES LOST IN TRANSIT

Where you are shipping pictures (as distinguished from undeveloped film), the same legal principles set forth above apply. The case is simpler in that you do not have to prove that the film was not defective, that the pictures were properly exposed, and that in all probability you would have had good pictures.

The proof of damages is the same as that involved in exposed but undeveloped film. You must prove the value of the pictures. Value is fixed at either market value or intrinsic value. If the pictures do not have a market value then you are entitled to recover the intrinsic value. In the Railway Express case the photographer produced records of previous sales of similar pictures from which a market value could be fixed. He was able to show that he sold a certain percentage of all pictures taken by him and proved the price of his average sale. The court applied the same percentage to the 43 lost transparencies and awarded the average price for each of the pictures within the allowable percentage.

But suppose the photographer cannot prove market value. What happens then? In 1900, a case was decided in New York involving the loss of a box of negatives of scenery taken in a foreign land and having no market value.[6] The court said:

> That those articles had no market value was quite clearly shown, and when that appeared the plaintiff was at liberty to give such other evidence as would assist the jury to assess the actual value. That was to be done by showing the nature of the property; the cost of obtaining the photographs; the purpose for which they were procured, and the difficulty of replacing them. The jury were also entitled to take into consideration the value of the property to the plaintiff . . .

> The fact that the negatives were not good ones, and were not well taken, was, of course, to be considered; but, in addition to that, the jury might also consider that when one has gone a long way to obtain photographs of the scenery of a foreign land which is difficult to reach, or where the photograph is of some incident which is not likely to be repeated, even a poor representation may be of considerable value, if a picture can be printed from it, because, as far as it goes, it is a correct representation of what occurred. All of these things were to be considered by the jury. We cannot say that the amount of the verdict which they rendered was improper.

From this decision, which is still the law, it may be observed that where the pictures have no market value, no rule can be laid down as to how the court will fix value. Each case depends on its own facts and all of the circumstances will be considered in arriving at a fair amount.

PICTURES SUBMITTED TO MAGAZINES

Where a magazine publishes the conditions under which it will receive pictures, the conditions will generally be binding upon the photographer who voluntarily submits his pictures to the magazine. If the magazine states that pictures are not returnable or that the publication will not be responsible for loss of the pictures, it can generally be stated that the photographer will have no legal remedy. Most magazines carry disclaimers of liability or limit their liability on contributions voluntarily submitted (that is, not submitted pursuant to a specific contract between author or photographer and publisher). In the absence of such a limitation of liability statement, a photographer who can prove that a publication actually received his pictures could recover the value of his pictures if lost, unless the publication could show that the loss was not due to its carelessness or negligence. In this connection the photographer is referred to the rules governing legal proof of value discussed earlier in this chapter.

When a photographer submits pictures to a contest, the rules of the contest will generally determine the extent of the obligation of the person sponsoring the contest in the event pictures are lost or damaged.

PICTURES SUBMITTED TO
PROSPECTIVE PURCHASERS

Under the Uniform Commercial Code, adopted throughout the United States, in the absence of a special agreement regarding returns, the risk of loss or damage to goods sold on approval (which would include pictures) does not fall upon the purchaser until acceptance (U.C.C. 2-327). It thus becomes important for the photographer who submits pictures on approval to include specific instructions for their return if not purchased—including a time limit and a method of return, such as registered mail, messenger, railway or air express—and to insure them at a stated value. The law says that after notification by the purchaser of his election to return, such return is at the seller's risk and expense, but the purchaser must follow any reasonable instructions. The instructions for return should be in writing and, if possible, set forth in a receipt, which the photographer should obtain for the pictures. It should be noted that although the law says that the expense of return is on the seller (the photographer), the parties may agree otherwise; therefore, when the pictures are submitted at the request of a prospective purchaser, the photographer may be in a better position to have the purchaser assume the expense of return and the insurance or even the risk of loss.

CHAPTER V

The Nude in Photography and the Law of Obscenity

IN NO OTHER AREA of law affecting photography have there been such vast and dramatic changes as in the law of obscenity. In the first edition of this book, we told a story about a photographer who, fascinated by a nude painting he had seen in a museum, reproduced the background and pose to create a photographic work of art. In our story, our hypothetical photographer sent his film away for processing but received, instead of the developed negatives and prints he was so eagerly awaiting, a polite letter telling him that his pictures could not be delivered because of the laws against obscenity. The photographer asked himself why the nude picture in the museum was "art" but a similar photograph was "obscene." Changes in the law that occurred between the first and later editions of the book prompted us to inform our readers in the later editions that the above story (which was our way of describing a common problem that plagued photographers just a few years ago) was no longer true. Since the third edition, court decisions have further expanded the area of pictures entitled to constitutional protection.

The problem of processing pictures of nudes or semi-nudes has eased considerably. Unless the photographs are "hard-core pornography" they would, in all likelihood, be processed and returned in routine fashion, without comment from the processor. This is a very dramatic and substantial change, which we will discuss later on.

The laws and postal regulations that render "obscene" pictures unmailable still exist.[1] Furthermore, the United States Supreme Court has recently upheld a 1967 law that permits any private citizen to stop mail order companies from sending advertisements that he considers "erotically arousing or sexually provocative," and this surely includes pictures. Some rather strange requests have resulted on the part of persons who have objected to "junk mail" of catalogues containing pictures of items such as girdles and bed sheets.

However, aside from this erotic mail curb law, where the recipient is the judge as to which mail is erotically arousing, the big news is in the definition of "obscene" that has been spelled out by the courts, particularly by the United States Supreme Court. This definition importantly affects what will happen under the many statutes dealing with obscenity. The New York statute, for example, makes it a criminal offense to possess an obscene picture with knowledge of its character, with the intent to sell, lend, distribute, give away, or even to show such picture.[2] The New York law also says that a person who possesses six or more similar obscene articles is presumed to possess them with intent to use them for an illegal purpose. Under another provision of the New York statute there is a penalty for distribution of objectionable matter to children less than 17 years of age.[3]

In the past, the Post Office has unofficially applied the criteria of (1) visible pubic hair or (2) a tendency to incite lustful or immoral thoughts or deeds as to pictures sent by mail. In either case the picture was considered obscene. Many times the problem of making an ultimate judgment as to obscenity was not reached because some processors of prints or transparencies would not send or deliver any nudes, except those made for scientific purposes.

But the courts have now forced the Post Office to take a much more liberal view, and the processors have tended to follow suit. The dramatic change in the policy of processors of film is reflected in the following informative and interesting quotation from a letter we received in April, 1970, from the Eastman Kodak Company stating its current position on the delivery of pictures of nudes, indecent posture and sexual activity:

Our primary objective has always been to handle the property and orders of customers in a manner fully in accord with the law. The Company's withholding of films because of their subject matter is ordinarily justified only when it is likely that our delivery of such films would violate the law. Legal prohibitions of this nature have been relaxed substantially in recent years by decisions of the United States Supreme Court. Pictures may no longer be withheld, for example, simply because of nudity or indecent posture.

As a result our policy may now be restated as follows:

(1) We *should* withhold pictures (whether movie or still), which graphically depict sexual activity, if we do not have good reason to believe in good faith that they are solely for the customer's own personal use.

(2) We *should not* withhold pictures (whether movie or still), even though graphically depicting sexual activity, if we have good reason to believe in good faith that they are solely for the customer's own personal use.

Exceptions to the prohibition set forth in (1) above will be considered when it is clear that the films are to be used for scientific, medical or legitimate artistic purposes. Such matters may be referred to the Legal Department for consideration.

As in the past, these principles have to do with films submitted for processing, the character of which cannot be known to us until processing has been completed. When pictures are received for printing or duplication, we reserve the right not to print or make duplicates, especially in quantity, even though we believe the pictures to be legally deliverable. Eastman Kodak Company is not interested in offering its facilities for the multiplication of pictures which are clearly offensive. We may advise prospective customers accordingly, at the same time returning the original pictures to them.

We hope that the above information will be of some help.

This is a very substantial change in the processor's policy concerning "questionable pictures." Formerly, pictures were withheld, whether or not nudity was involved, if they were considered "dirty" or such as to incite immoral thoughts or deeds, and pictures depicting sexual activity were definitely withheld. This has now changed, except for that class of picture depicting sexual and other activity that falls into the category of hard-core pornography.

The pendulum having now swung to the other extreme, it is appropriate to discuss the decisions of the courts during the last few years to attain a better understanding of how far the cases go in defining what is and what is not obscene. Although the United States

Supreme Court has taken a liberal view in keeping with the change of attitudes toward sex and nudity, we must emphasize that in 1969 and 1970 several new judges ascended to that court, and it is entirely conceivable that some of the liberal views expressed by the former majority may not necessarily reflect the view of the new majority. It is true that the court generally follows its previous decisions, but every new case is decided on its own facts, and the court is always free to refuse to follow a precedent that it thinks is no longer valid.

To say to the photographer that "anything goes" is far from accurate, and photographers must be warned that in spite of the vast liberalization in the law regarding obscene pictures, the law still does not tolerate hard-core pornography (which, as will be seen later on, is not an easy term to define, although the legal tests for determining it have been spelled out). We shall try to trace the development of the law during recent years to show the gradual transition from the previously prevailing views denouncing a picture of a nude to the present stage where even pictures of sexual activity in certain instances are accorded constitutional protection.

For a long time the courts have held that nudity itself was not necessarily obscene, and that the sale of pictures of nudes and semi-nudes does not in and of itself constitute a violation of law. The courts, in making pronouncements on the question of obscenity, have sometimes said that the test is whether the tendency of the material is to deprave or corrupt, whether its motive is pure or impure, or whether it is naturally calculated to excite impure imagination or lustful thoughts. But the United States Supreme Court has said that because suppressing free speech and press (and photographs are surely included here) involves an important guarantee of the First Amendment, the definitions used in the statutes which make any form of expression unlawful must be very clear and definite, so that people will know what is permitted and what is forbidden. In a series of cases involving motion pictures, the Supreme Court declared that such standards for restraint or punishment as "sexual immorality,"[4] "immoral,"[5] "harmful,"[6] and "prejudicial to the best interests of the people of said City"[7] are too vague and uncertain to be used in deciding whether or not a motion picture could, under the Constitution, be withheld from the public. In *Roth v. United States,* a 1957 case involving the sale of allegedly obscene books and phonograph records, the Supreme Court stated what it thought was the proper definition for the kind of material that could properly be excluded from the protection afforded free speech and press under the First Amendment to the Constitution of the United States.[8] The Court said that the test of obscenity is:

> Whether to the average person, applying contemporary standards, the dominant theme of the material taken as a whole appeals to prurient interest.

As we shall see, however, this definition has been considerably expanded and broadened in the past 13 years.

In 1961, the Supreme Court spoke again on the definition of obscenity, clarifying, in an opinion by Justice Harlan, the definition handed down in Roth.[9] The case, *Manual v. Day,* involved a ruling of the Post Office Department, sustained both by the District Court and the Court of Appeals, barring from the mails a shipment of magazines containing the photographs of nude, or near-nude male models, together with the models' names and addresses. The Supreme Court reversed the decision of the lower courts, and Justice Harlan said:

> ... The question whether these magazines are "obscene," as it was decided below and argued before us, was thought to depend solely on a determination as to the relevant "audience" in terms of which their "prurient interest" appeal should be judged. This view of the obscenity issue evidently stemmed from the belief that in *Roth v. United States,* 354 U.S. 476, 480, this Court established the following *single* test for determining whether challenged material is obscene: "whether to the average person, applying contemporary community standards, the dominant theme of the material taken as a whole appeals to prurient interest." ... On this basis the Court of Appeals, rejecting the petitioners' contention that the "prurient interest" appeal of the magazines should be judged in terms of their likely impact on the "average person," even though not a likely recipient of the magazines, held that the administrative finding respecting their impact on the "average homosexual" sufficed to establish the Government's case as to their obscenity.

We do not reach the question thus thought below to be dispositive on this aspect of the case. For we find lacking in these magazines an element which, no less than "prurient interest," is essential to a valid determination of obscenity. . . . These magazines cannot be deemed so offensive on their face as to affront current community standards of decency — a quality that we shall hereafter refer to as "patent offensiveness" or "indecency." Lacking that quality, the magazines cannot be deemed legally "obscene" and we need not consider the question of the proper "audience" by which their "prurient interest" appeal should be judged. . . .

Obscenity under the federal statute requires proof of two distinct elements: (1) patent offensiveness; and (2) "prurient interest" appeal. Both must conjoin before challenged material can be found "obscene" under §1461." . . .

To consider that the "obscenity" exception in "the area of constitutionally protected speech or press," *Roth*, at 485, does not require any determination as to the patent offensiveness of the material itself might well put the American public in jeopardy of being denied access to many worthwhile works in literature, science, or art. For one would not have to travel far even among the acknowledged masterpieces in any of these fields to find works whose "dominant theme" might, not beyond reason, be claimed to appeal to the "prurient interest" of the reader or observer. We decline to attribute to Congress any such quixotic and deadening purpose as would bar from the mails all material, not patently offensive, which stimulates impure desires relating to sex.

From the above you can see that a picture is not obscene merely because it portrays a nude, male or female, or merely because it may lead to "impure sexual thoughts." It must be "patently offensive" and "the dominant theme of the material taken as a whole" must appeal to "prurient interest" of the average person, applying contemporary standards. The Supreme Court in that case, however, refused to decide two questions: whether the particular "audience" to which a publication is addressed should determine what standards should be applied, and whether these two tests limit "obscene" material to hard-core pornography only. Let us talk a moment about the second question. "Hard-core pornography" has sometimes been described as material with "prurient" or sexual interest which is so clearly offensive and candid that it would be termed "lewd" or "dirty" no matter what set of "contemporary community standards" was applied. Some courts have said that the Supreme Court definitions of obscenity, properly interpreted, have indeed limited the powers of the courts to restrict, on the basis of "obscenity," only hard-core pornography.[10] This statement has not been universally accepted, however, and it can be expected that some courts (and some prosecutors) will continue to find "obscene" certain material which does not *quite* meet the definition of hard-core pornography. For this reason, although most nude photographs should be considered freely mailable, processors may be justified in refusing to handle material which borders on the pornographic.

If we return to the first question we mentioned as not having been decided by the Supreme Court in the *Manual v. Day* case, we will be talking about a matter which has received considerable attention from the courts in the past, and which has been important in determining whether a particular expression, literary or photographic, could be seized (or the authors or distributors punished) because it was "immoral" or "obscene," etc. In one case, for example,[11] the condemned pictures were found on a magazine rack in a candy store. They consisted of pictures published in sets displaying a strip tease. The models were shown in various stages until complete nudity was achieved. The court noted that the defendant was the manager of a candy store who sold sets of pictures indiscriminately to anyone who desired to purchase them and emphasized the fact that this would hardly be considered a channel through which actual students of art usually buy their material. The court commented:

> Let us look at this case with a realistic approach. Here is a small neighborhood store serving the families of the area. It caters to high school children who come in, observe these pictures, purchase them and seek dark corners and privacy to snicker over its contents and pass the pictures around among their friends.

Here it might be noted that under certain statutes, similar to the New York Penal Law referred to in the early part of this chapter, there is a penalty for distribution of objectionable matter to children under 17 years of age. Pictures that do not meet the tests of obscenity in the case of an adult might very well constitute "objectionable matter" when distributed to a minor, thus subjecting the seller to prosecution.

In another case,[12] "frankly provocative" nude pictures were sold in a store specializing in magic and novelty articles but the windows featured art books containing nudes. In another prosecution,[13] some of the pictures featured two or more models in various poses in the nude. They were sold in a bookstore specializing in the sale of cheap books. In still another case,[14] the pictures were purchased at a bookstore which from its window display featured sexy books with titles such as *Free Lovers, Sinful Cities of the Western World, How To Make Love,* and others. The last three cases mentioned were all tried at one time. The court in deciding against the sellers said that in determining whether the pictures are obscene within the law one can start with the proposition that nudity *per se* is not obscenity. But the judge then went on to say when one sees men pawing over such pictures in stores in the Times Square area, it is obvious that their appeal is frankly sexual and that the pictures in question, therefore, meet the test of obscenity.

Anyone who is familiar with the Times Square area at this time, however, is appalled by the multitude of stores, which have mushroomed in this area, that display and sell books and pictures dealing with sex in all its forms.

As we said above, this is the way that cases of this kind tended to be decided in the past — the court would look at the place and at the community where the pictures were sold and at least partly on this basis would decide whether they were obscene. However, there has now been a decision, handed down within the last few months in the United States Supreme Court in the case of *Jacobellis v. Ohio*[15] which settles in quite another way the question of what community standards are to be applied in determining obscenity.

The Jacobellis case involved the French motion picture *Les Amants (The Lovers)*. Nico Jacobellis, manager of a motion picture theatre in Cleveland Heights, Ohio, showed *The Lovers* in his theatre and was convicted on two counts for possessing and exhibiting an obscene film in violation of Ohio law. His conviction was affirmed by one appellate court and then affirmed again by the Supreme Court of Ohio. In reversing the Ohio courts, the

Supreme Court said that it was holding to the decision in the Roth case that we talked about earlier in this chapter, and quoted from that decision a statement that obscenity is excluded from constitutional protection only because it is "utterly without redeeming social importance."

The Jacobellis case brought into issue whether local community standards should be applied in determining obscenity, or whether there should be some sort of national standard, with the United States being considered the "community." The Supreme Court, in an opinion written by Justice Brennan, said that local standards may not be applied. Justice Brennan said:

> It has been suggested that the "contemporary community standards" aspect of the *Roth* test implies a determination of the constitutional question of obscenity in each case by the standards of the particular local community from which the case arises. This is an incorrect reading of Roth. . . .
>
> We do not see how any "local" definition of the "community" could properly be employed in delineating the area of expression that is protected by the Federal Constitution. Mr. Justice Harlan pointed out in *Manual Enterprises, Inc. v. Day* . . . that a standard based on a particular local community would have "the intolerable consequence of denying some sections of the country access to material, there deemed acceptable, which in others might be considered offensive to prevailing community standards of decency. Cf. *Butler v. Michigan,* 352 U.S. 380. It is true that *Manual Enterprises* dealt with the federal statute banning obscenity from the mails. But the mails are not the only means by which works of expression cross local-community lines in this country. It can hardly be assumed that all patrons of a particular library, bookstand, or motion picture theatre are residents of the smallest local "community" that can be drawn around that establishment. Furthermore, to sustain the suppression of a particular book or film in one locality would deter its dissemination in other localities where it might be held not obscene, since sellers and exhibitors would be reluctant to risk criminal conviction in testing the variation between the two places. It would be a hardy person who would sell a book or exhibit a film anywhere in the land after this Court had sustained the judgment of one "community" holding it to be outside the constitutional protection. The result would thus be "to restrict the public's access to forms of the printed word which the State could not constitutionally suppress directly. *Smith v. California,* 361 U.S. 147, 154. . . .
>
> We recognize the legitimate and indeed exigent interest of States and localities throughout the Nation in preventing the dissemination

of material deemed harmful to children. But that interest does not justify a total suppression of such material, the effect of which would be to "reduce the adult population . . . to reading only what is fit for children." *Butler v. Michigan,* 352 U.S. 380, 383. State and local authorities might well consider whether their objectives in this area would be better served by laws aimed specifically at preventing distribution of objectionable material to children, rather than at totally prohibiting its dissemination. Since the present conviction is based upon exhibition of the film to the public at large and not upon its exhibition to children, the judgment must be reviewed under the strict standard applicable in determining the scope of the expression that is protected by the Constitution.

We have applied that standard to the motion picture in question. *The Lovers* involves a woman bored with her life and marriage who abandons her husband and family for a young archaeologist with whom she has suddenly fallen in love. There is an explicit love scene in the last reel of the film, and the State's objections are based almost entirely upon that scene. . . . We have viewed the film, in the light of the record made in the trial court, and we conclude that it is not obscene within the standards enunciated in *Alberts v. California* and *Roth v. United States,* which we reaffirm here.

Therefore, the Supreme Court has said that whether a thing is obscene must be judged by a general standard which applies throughout the country and not according to such factors as the particular community or, in our opinion, the particular audience involved.

It can be anticipated that some local police and prosecuting authorities may be slow to follow this decision in its fullest implications, because it reduces the area of activity for which obscenity prosecutions are possible to a very narrow area indeed. Indeed, Justice Stewart, who wrote a separate concurring opinion in this case, said that he had reached the conclusion, on the basis of the Supreme Court cases, that under the First and Fourteenth Amendments criminal obscenity laws are constitutionally limited to hard-core pornography.

Considering now some of the cases decided since the last edition of our book which point to the dramatic change in the law of obscenity, we find a good discussion of the law in a decision of the New York Criminal Court handed down in January, 1969, in the case of *People v. Stabile,* 296 N.Y.S. 2d 815. The defendants were charged with selling obscene magazines containing single photographs of females in various poses and stages of nudity, some provocative and prominently displaying the vaginal aperture but not depicting any sexual activity. The court held that the magazines were protected by the First and Fourteenth Amendments of the United States Constitution (freedom of press) in the absence of violation of laws concerning protection of juveniles (a state may constitutionally establish two standards of obscenity, one for minors and one for adults), or in the absence of foisting such material on an unwilling public or resorting to "pandering" methods in distribution.

Judge Ringel's opinion in the *Stabile* case contains such an excellent discussion of the law that we quote it practically in its entirety as follows:

"There are two judicially approved tests for obscenity—the Federal test, and the New York State test.

"A. The Federal Test

"The Federal test, sometimes called the 'prurient interest' or 'Roth' test (*Roth v. United States,* supra) applied in the Federal courts, fixes the *minimum* standards that a state may employ in judging publications for obscenity.

"This test provided '. . . whether to the average person, applying contemporary community standards, the dominant theme of the material taken as a whole appeals to prurient interest' (*Roth,* ibid at p. 489, 77 S.Ct. 1304, at p. 1311).

"The test was amended in 1966 in three cases, *Ginzburg v. United States* (383 U.S. 463, 86 S.Ct. 942, 16 L.Ed. 2d 31), *Mishkin v. New York,* 383 U.S. 502, 86 Ct. 958, 16 L.Ed. 2d 56 and the *'Fanny Hill'* case, *A Book Named 'John Cleland's Memoirs of a Woman of Pleasure' v. Attorney General of Massachusetts* (383 U.S. 413, 86 S.Ct. 975, 16 L.Ed. 2d 1).

"In *Ginzburg,* the Court held that when an objective examination of the material in question fails to establish obscenity, then the Court may examine into the publisher's intent and in that connection may consider the advertising material he issued in connection with the material under review. If the publisher attempted to 'titilate' the sexual interests of the public in an effort to sell his product, then the Courts may consider his advertising 'at its face value' and declare the publication obscene.

"In *Mishkin,* the Court held that a publication aimed at deviant sexual groups is obscene if it appeals to the prurient interest of those groups.

"In *'Fanny Hill'* the Court held under this definition, as elaborated in subsequent cases, three elements must coalesce; it must be established that (a) the dominant theme of the material taken as a whole appeals to a prurient interest in sex; (b) the material is patently offensive because it affronts contemporary community standards relating to the description or representation of sexual matters; and (c) the material is 'utterly without redeeming social value' (383 U.S. at p. 418, 86 S.Ct. 975 at p. 977).

" *'Fanny Hill'* thus modified *Roth* by requiring that a publication must be *utterly* without redeeming social value before it could be proscribed. Nevertheless, if the book was 'designed for and primarily disseminated to a clearly defined deviant sexual group, rather than the public at large,' it may likewise be proscribed (*Mishkin,* at p. 508, 86 S.Ct. 958, at p. 963).

"[3] The term 'contemporary community standards' must be interpreted in a parochial sense but is equated with the contemporary community standards of the nation as a whole since the area of expression that is protected is governed by the Federal Constitution (*Jacobellis v. Ohio,* supra, at p. 193, 84 S.Ct. 1676).

" *'Fanny Hill'* was followed by *Redrup v. New York* [1967] (386 U.S. 767, 87 S.Ct. 1414). In effect, *Redrup* holds material to be obscene if it is hard-core pornography, *and* in 'borderline' cases, the publication may be proscribed if (a) it is sold to a minor in violation of some local statute . . . *or* (b) if it is pandered . . . *or,* (c) if it is foisted upon an unwilling public . . . .

"Any doubt as to the meaning of *Redrup* is resolved in *Central Magazine Sales, Ltd. v. United States* [1967] (389 U.S. 50, 88 S.Ct. 235, 19 L.Ed. 2d 49). *Central Sales* involved a magazine called *'Exclusive'* which contained a collection of photographs of females in various stages of nudity, and some of which are posed in such a manner as 'to reveal the genital area in its entirety.' There was also some suggestion of masochism in some of the photographs. Although the trial court found the magazine to be obscene (*United States v. 392 Copies of a Magazine Entitled Exclusive,* 253 F.Supp. 485), which determination was affirmed on appeal (373 F. 2d 633), nevertheless, the United States Supreme Court reversed without opinion, per curiam, citing only *Redrup.*

"In many other recent cases the United States Supreme Court has likewise summarily reversed, without opinion, federal and state court findings of obscenity as to magazines showing photographs of nude or semi-nude males or females which focused on the genitalia. In each of these cases *Redrup* was the authority cited . . . .

"The term 'hard-core' pornography is an imprecise term. In his dissent in *Jacobellis v. Ohio,* supra, at p. 197, 84 S.Ct. 1676, at p. 1683, Mr. Justice Stewart stated '. . . perhaps I could never succeed in intelligibly' defining that term, 'but I know it when I see it.' However, in a subsequent dissenting opinion (*Ginzburg v. United States,* supra, at p. 499, 86 S.Ct. 942, at p. 957, f. n. 3) he set forth what he meant by that term:

" '. . . Such materials include photographs, both still and motion picture, with no pretense of artistic value, graphically depicting acts of sexual intercourse, including various acts of sodomy and sadism, and sometimes involving several participants in scenes of orgy-like character. They also include strips of drawings in comicbook format grossly depicting similar activities in an exaggerated fashion . . . .'

"B. The New York Test

"In interpreting former New York Penal Law, section 1141, the New York Court of Appeals held that it 'should apply only to what may properly be termed "hard-core pornography." ' (*People v. Richmond County News* [1961], 9 N.Y. 2d 578, 586, 216 N.Y.S. 2d 369, 375, 175 N.E. 2d 681.) Although many people may know it when they see it, the term was never defined by the Court other than to say that the test 'may be applied objectively.' . . . The test is far less stringent than the federal test which, as noted above, is subjective and consists of the prurient appeal—patently offensive—utterly without redeeming social value elements (*Roth,* supra; '*Fanny*

Hill,' supra; McKinney's Penal Law, Book 39, Part 2, Practice Commentary, p. 89).

"[4] However, by enacting Revised Penal Law § 235.00 the New York State Legislature has now adopted the federal definition of obscenity as expressed in *'Fanny Hill,'* supra, thus eliminating the single hard-core pornography test laid down in *Richmond County News,* supra.

"[5] Under either test, if the material is hard-core pornography, it is not protected. . . . In this Court's view, pictures of nudes, absent any indication of sexual activity, are not hard-core (see *Ginzburg v. United States,* p. 499, 86 S.Ct. 942, f. n. 3, supra, dissent, Stewart J.).

"Although *People v. G.I. Distributors, Inc.* (20 N.Y. 2d 104, 281 N.Y.S. 2d 795, 228 N.E. 2d 787) was decided under former Penal Law § 1141, the definition of hard-core indicated therein is significant. 'Photographs of similar *sexual activity* between male and female, without social justification or excuse, would be equally obscene.' . . . In *People v. Noroff,* 67 Cal. 2d 791, 63 Cal.Rptr. 575, 433 P. 2d 479, supra, the Supreme Court of California found the publication *International Nudist Sun,* Vol. 1, No. 5, constitutionally protected because . . . 'none of the photographs display any form of *sexual activity.'* . . . In the same opinion . . . the Court noted, 'The graphic depiction of such sexual activity seems to be the distinguishing feature of the only materials which the United States Supreme Court has ever ruled obscene.'

"Note also, that in his dissent in *G. I. Distributors,* supra, Chief Judge Fuld voted to reverse, inter alia, because 'there is neither indecent exposure nor portrayal of a consummated lewd act.' . . .

"Addressing ourselves to the *'Fanny Hill'* test, we conclude that the Federal and New York State tests are now the same (McKinney's Consol. Laws, Penal Law Book 39, Part 2, Penal Law [1968], Commission Staff Notes, Article 235 § 235.00). This means that *Redrup,* supra, and *'Fanny Hill,'* supra, are controlling here.

"[6, 7] 'Sex and obscenity are not synonymous' (*Roth v. United*

States, p. 487, 77 S.Ct. p. 1310, supra). Accordingly, absent '. . . a claim that the statute in question reflected a specific and limited state concern for juveniles. See *Prince v. Massachusetts,* 321 U.S. 158, 64 S.Ct. 438, 88 L.Ed. 645; cf. *Butler v. Michigan,* 352 U.S. 380, 77 S.Ct. 524, 1 L.Ed. 2d 412'; *or* 'any suggestion of an assault upon individual privacy by publication in a manner so obtrusive as to make it impossible for an unwilling individual to avoid exposure to it (cf. *Breard v. City of Alexandria,* 341 U.S. 622, 71 S.Ct. 920, 95 L.Ed. 1233) . . .'; *or* evidence of the sort of 'pandering' which the Court found significant in *Ginzburg v. United States.* . . . it must be concluded that the distribution of the material in question is protected by the First and Fourteenth Amendments.

"It is to be noted that many courts have held to the same effect with respect to similar or identical photographs as are before the Court. See *People v. Liebowitz* (App. Term, New York State Supreme Court) . . . .

"[8] What may be 'clearly obscene in the ordinary sense of the word' does not necessarily make a publication obscene as a matter of law (*United States v. 4,440 Copies etc.,* 276 F.Supp. 902, 903, supra). It is to be observed that in this case the Court reviewed photographs of women in various suggestive poses which exposed to open view their breasts and vaginas and were 'lewder than any magazines heretofore considered' by that Court.

"Note too that the United States Supreme Court has held, in a case where the defendants conceded that magazines of nude males were without literary merit and were prepared for homosexuals, that the magazines were not legally obscene as there is an absence of 'patent offensiveness' or 'indecency' on the face of the photographs so as to affront current community standards of decency . . . .

"In summary, the following conclusions may be drawn from the various decisions:

"[9] (1) A State may constitutionally establish two standards of obscenity—one for juveniles and one for adults. (*Redrup,* supra; *People v. Tannenbaum,* supra)

"(2) The Federal and New York State tests for obscenity are identical.

"(3) Obscene material enjoys no constitutional protection. It is contraband. (*Roth v. United States,* supra)

"[10] (4) Hard-core pornography is obscene under both Federal and New York law. (*Redrup,* supra; *People v. Noroff,* supra)

"[11] (5) Motion pictures, like books, are entitled to the protection of the First Amendment and the three-fold test stated in *'Fanny Hill'* is applicable to both. (*I Am Curious—Yellow,* supra)

"[12] (6) The 'prurient appeal' test of *'Fanny Hill'* includes prurient appeal to sexually deviant groups. (*Mishkin v. New York,* supra)

"[13] Photographs of nudes depicting sexual activity are 'hardcore.' (*G.I. Distributors, Inc.,* supra)

"[14] Sex and obscenity are not synonymous. Thus, the distribution of photographs depicting genitalia (the so-called close cases; see *Ginzburg,* supra, at p. 474, 86 S.Ct. 942), which are not 'hard-core,' is protected by the First and Fourteenth Amendments, unless (1) they are distributed to juveniles in violation of some statute, *or* (2) they are foisted upon an unwilling public in violation of one's right to privacy, *or* (3) they are 'pandered.' (*Redrup,* supra)

"[15] Also, in close cases, the publisher's advertising 'blurbs' may be considered in determining the question of obscenity. (*Ginzburg v. United States,* supra)

"[16] In our view, the term 'close cases' refers to material, which on objective examination, standing alone, is not patently offensive, i.e., hard-core pornography (*Richmond County News,* supra). More particularly, the term applies to that material in which some, but not all of the three elements of the three-fold test enunciated in *'Fanny Hill'* are present. (*I Am Curious—Yellow,* supra, p. 200 concurring opinion, Friendly, J.)

"We conclude, therefore, that while 'hard-core pornography' is obscene per se and does not enjoy any constitutional protection (*Roth,* supra), 'close cases' are to be adjudged as either obscene vel non, depending upon whether the material violates the tests pronounced in *Redrup,* supra.

"This determination is supported by the decision *I Am Curious—Yellow,* supra. That case concerned the showing of a motion picture which depicted scenes of a young girl and her lover nude, sexual intercourse, and oral-genital activity. Although the Court (p. 198) found that 'the sexual content of the film is presented with greater explicitness than has been seen in any other film produced for general viewing,' [yet] taken as a whole, it was an artistic presentation of a young girl's search for identity. The Court thereupon concluded that, taken as a whole, the film does not appeal 'to prurient interest in sex,' and 'is [not] utterly without redeeming social value.' Thus, 'it falls within the ambit of intellectual effort that the first amendment was designed to protect.' (pp. 199-200) Accordingly, absent the existence of two of the elements of the three-fold test enunciated in *'Fanny Hill,'* supra, the picture was not obscene.

"Apparently, mindful of *Redrup,* supra, the Court warned the importers, distributors and exhibitors that if they failed to exclude minors from the audience they would be subject to attack under *Ginsberg v. New York* (390 U.S. 629, 88 S.Ct. 1274, 20 L.Ed. 2d 195 [1968], and if they 'pandered' the film, then *Ginzburg v. United States* (383 U.S. 463, 86 S.Ct. 942, L.Ed. 2d 31 [1966], supra, would be applicable (*United States v. I Am Curious—Yellow,* 404 F. 2d 196, 200, supra, concurring opinion, Friendly, J.)

"[17] The rule enunciated in *Redrup* (supra) is consonant with the First and Fourteenth Amendments in that it protects the average normal adult in his right to read, view and hear what he pleases. Any other rule would reduce the rights of adults to read, view and hear only what is fit for children . . . .

"The material before the Court is coarse, puerile, offensive and distasteful. But these elements alone do not render it obscene under the law or proscribable.

"[18] '[T]he price of freedom of religion or of speech or of the press is that we must put up with, and even pay for a good deal of rubbish.' (*United States v. Ballard,* 322 U.S. 78, at p. 95 . . .)

"In view of the authorities cited herein, defendants' motion to dismiss, as a matter of law, are granted."

In dealing with pictures depicting sexual activity we see that the courts have granted constitutional protection to moving pictures of sexual intercourse and oral-genital activity in the *I Am Curious—*

Yellow case on the ground that, taken as a whole, it is not utterly without redeeming social value. However, this does not mean that separate photographs of sexual activity will receive similar protection.

In *Cohen v. Carroll,* decided in the New York City Criminal Court in April, 1970, the police seized 48 separate photographs of males and females in acts of sexual intercourse of manifold variety. The court said:

> Not mere nudity was depicted in these photographs, which is not now proscribed . . . but provocative, lewd and lascivious intercourse. . . . which is [proscribed] . . . .
>
> These respondents were engaged in the business of purveying . . . graphic matter . . . to appeal to the erotic interests of their customers. They were plainly engaged in the commercial exploitation of the morbid and shameful craving for materials with prurient effect . . . . Respondents do not come into court as the champions of a brave new permissive sexual philosophy but solely as salesman against a background of commercial exploitation of erotica solely for the sake of their prurient appeal.

Notwithstanding the *Fanny Hill, I Am Curious—Yellow, The Lovers* and other cases referred to above, we still find courts differing in their application of the three-fold test in the case of motion pictures. We have seen where Justice Brennan, writing for the United States Supreme Court in the *Jacobellis (The Lovers)* case, held that the "explicit love scene" in the last reel of the film does not render the motion picture obscene.

Yet in *Hosey v. City of Jackson,* 309 F. Supp. 527, decided in January, 1970, the United States District Court in Mississippi held that the motion picture *Candy* was devoid of literary or artistic merit, presented nothing more than a vivid portrayal of hard-core pornography, and was without redeeming social value. The court in the *Candy* film case said:

> This film has no discernible theme or plot and involves a disconnected series of scenes depicting sexual gratification in a shocking and shameful manner. The Court certainly concurs with the observations of defendants' witness Dean John S. Jenkins who testified:

"The film is in my opinion a series of unrelated sequences in the life of this girl and each of the scenes builds up to the disrobing of the female and then the filming of various forms of sexual activity with her. In my opinion these scenes are clearly designed to arouse what we might consider normal, as well as abnormal, interest and emotions in sexual behavior." (Jenkins Dep. pp. 5-6)

The defendants categorize the film as a satire or a spoof on various aspects of modern life. Such a categorization, however, does not bring this obscene film within the constitutional protection of the First Amendment. The graphic portrayal of illicit, unnatural and incestuous sexual relationships which dominate the entirety of this film leave little to the imagination and completely overpowers or minimizes the presence of any elements of satire.

This motion picture is violative of the tridentated test as enunciated in *Memoirs,* supra, in that the dominant theme of the material in this film taken as a whole appeals to a prurient interest in sex, the material is patently offensive because it clearly affronts contemporary community standards relating to the representation of sexual matters, and the material is utterly without redeeming social value. All three of these elements coalesce when applied to the film *Candy.* It is necessary for one to view the various lurid and bizarre activities depicted in this film and hear the sound effects incidental thereto in order to fully appreciate the obscene and disgusting nature of this motion picture in its entirety.

In *McGrew v. City of Jackson,* 307 F.Supp. 754, decided in December, 1969, the same Mississippi District Court found the motion picture *The Fox* to be obscene. In comparing it with *The Lovers,* which was held not to be obscene in the *Jacobellis* case, the court said:

The film protected [in] *Jacobellis v. State of Ohio,* 378 U.S. 184, 84 S.Ct. 1676, 12 L.Ed. 2d 793 (*The Lovers*), [was] reviewed by the Supreme Court, which said that the reel involved an affair between a woman bored with her marriage who had abandoned her husband for a younger man and that the last reel most severely criticized simply displayed "an explicit love scene." That nicety of characterization simply does not fit as a description of the lurid and carnal scenes in *The Fox* which so far exceeded all bounds of propriety and common decency by any standards. *The Fox* is a classic case of hard core pornography wherein sex is pandered solely for profit.

It should be noted that in both the *Candy* and *The Fox* cases there were dissenting opinions by one of the judges, who declared in the latter case:

Following the precedent set in *Entertainment Ventures Inc., et al. v. Brewer, et al,* supra, I would have preferred simply to rule on the constitutionality of the pertinent state statute and the constitutionality of the arrests of the plaintiffs and of the seizure of the film. We might then have foregone viewing the movie. However, since we have now witnessed the showing of the film, I would express my agreement with the declaration of Chief Judge William C. Keady.

"That the motion picture *The Fox* is hereby declared not to be obscene, in fact or in law, in accordance with controlling decisions, particularly *Roth v. United States of America,* 354 U.S. 476 [77 S.Ct. 1304] 1 L.Ed. 1498, and *Jacobellis v. Ohio,* 378 U.S. 184, [84 S.Ct. 1676] 12 L.Ed. 2d. 793 . . . ."

For the foregoing reasons, I respectfully dissent.

In an earlier case, *Ratner v. Widdle,* 307 F. Supp. 471, decided in April, 1968, the United States District Court in California held as obscene a motion picture dealing with the subject of flagellation, saying:

The subject film portrayed, to an *ad nauseam* extent, the enthusiastic striking of the "bare behinds" of young women with the use of the open hand, cane, paddle and bullwhip, the last mentioned weapon having been applied indiscriminately to virtually all parts of the mostly undraped figure. The performance was completely candid in portraying what was involved, it also reflected a revolting desecration of the human body. It is particularly in this latter respect that it seems to me to go beyond the acceptable standards that govern the three tests of obscenity (and the test of candor as well, if that is a separate guide).

In *People v. Steinberg,* a New York case, decided in October, 1969, 304 N.Y.S. 2d 858, the County Court of Westchester County found to be obscene motion pictures with such titles as *The Girl from Pussycat, Professor Lust* and similar titles. In rejecting the argument of defendant that every film has redeeming social importance and that erotic motion pictures have as much right to the protection of the First Amendment as does *Chitty Chitty Bang Bang,* the court said:

Non obscene films do, but obscene films are not within the protection afforded by the First Amendment. *Roth,* supra. Defendants further seek a determination that the Supreme Court standards which are, in fact continuously troublesome be set aside in the interests of logic and common sense. This Court feels that the application of logic and common sense by the Courts of this State and nation to questions involving films of this type might well result in proscribing this type of film as well as the other filth and depravity which prey on society as a whole in the interests of a small group of smut peddlers intent upon pecuniary profits. This Court has obligations to all the people of this county and to ignore the exhibition of this type of gross depravity under the guise of free speech in the interest of commercial exploitation would be a dereliction of its duty to the People.

We have thus seen that pictures of sexual activity, when part of a motion picture, are examined in the light of the entire story in applying the three-fold test stated in the *Jacobellis, Fanny Hill* and *I Am Curious—Yellow* cases in determining whether they are to be adjudged obscene.

Motion pictures also use the pedantic approach to the subject of illustrating sexual relations as an aid to a happy marriage, which although not presented in story-type fashion, would also be accorded constitutional protection. Among the recent pictures are *Marital Fulfillment, The Art of Marriage* and *Man and Wife.* The same applies to books containing pictures on the subject. However, such pictures sold separately by those engaged in the commercial exploitation of erotica solely for the sake of prurient appeal still face the danger of prosecution as was seen in the *Cohen v. Carroll* case.

We have also seen from the *People v. Stabile* case that magazines showing single pictures of females in various poses and stages of nudity, some provocatively displaying the vaginal aperture but no *sexual activity,* have been accorded constitutional protection even though "coarse, puerile, offensive and distasteful."

What the future holds in store for the sex movies, books and magazines that are inundating our society in this age of the sex revolution and sexual permissiveness we cannot predict.

The Commission on Obscenity and Pornography recently concluded public hearings before the House Judiciary Committee in Washington on anti-obscenity legislation to determine what new laws, if any, should be recommended. One of the final witnesses, who was the project coordinator of the Underground Press Syndicate, disrupted the hearing by placing a cheese pie on the head of one of the Commission members and exclaiming "pie power" as the solution to pomposity. We hardly recommend this as a means of preventing anti-obscenity legislation.

Whether the present liberal views on obscenity will continue in accordance with the principles previously discussed or whether there will be future legislation creating new definitions we do not know. It is fair to state, however, that there appears to be very little left that is "obscene" under the law short of pictures of sexual activities, which do not fall within the protected area noted above.

But we caution photographers not to be misled into thinking that pictures of anything short of sexual activities are safe, especially where the mail is involved. For example, in a recent Federal court case, reported in May, 1970, (*U.S. v. Wild,* 422 F. 2d 34), defendants operating a mail order business were convicted of sending obscene matter through the mail. The Circuit Court of Appeals upheld the conviction. The report of the case states the holding as follows:

> The Court of Appeals, Lumbard, Chief Judge, held that slides depicting nude male, seated or lying facing camera, holding or touching his erect penis or depicting two nude males in act of fellatio constituted hard core pornography . . . .

Those who have the time and means can appeal convictions to higher courts in the hope of getting a reversal; as stated in the early part of this chapter, however, changes in the make up of the majority of the United States Supreme Court may result in a second look at the liberal views presently existing.

By way of postscript to the *Ginzburg* case referred to in this chapter, it might be noted that a Federal court judge has just reduced Ginzburg's sentence from five to three years. Ginzburg was convicted in 1963 for sending obscene materials through the mail. The case became a cause célèbre when the United States Supreme Court upheld the conviction, not on the ground that the publications were obscene but because promotion of them pandered to prurient interests. At the rehearing for reconsideration of his sentence, his attorneys argued that times had changed since his conviction in 1963 and that book shops and newsstands surrounding the Courthouse now sold books and magazines that made Ginzburg's publications look tame by comparison. His attorneys also argued that since the time the Supreme Court had upheld the conviction it had reversed 16 obscenity convictions in which the publications were overwhelmingly more offensive than Ginzburg's. (*New York Times,* May 27, 1970)

In closing, we might also add by way of consolation to photographers that most of the prosecutions have been against sellers and distributors of the material, although photographers are not immune.

CHAPTER VI

Copyright

WHEN PHOTOGRAPHY WAS still an infant art — twenty-six years after Daguerre's "first practical application of photography"[1] in 1839 — the Congress of the United States decided that photography was entitled to specific copyright protection. In 1865, an amendment to the United States copyright law stated that the provisions of the Copyright Act "shall extend to and include photographs and the negatives thereof which shall hereafter be made."[2] From the standpoint of photographers, however, and despite this early recognition by Congress, the subject of copyright protection for their pictures has always seemed a difficult area. One of the problems is that copyright law is quite complex. Another problem has been cost — each separate copyright registration costs $4.00. If it were necessary to register separately each picture for which protection was desired, this would be too expensive even for the most successful photographers — and all the methods for avoiding the $4.00 per picture charge, discussed later in this chapter, involve additional steps in handling the pictures, added legal complications, or both. Photographic societies, as well as publishers in this field, have continued to press for an easier and cheaper — and therefore more effective — means of securing adequate copyright protection for photographers.

Why is such protection so important to the photographer? What does it mean to have a copyright on a photograph, and what does it mean not to have one?

BASIC PRINCIPLES

Basically, copyright is that area of the law which is concerned with the exclusive right of authors, artists, photographers and others to use and reproduce that which they have created. When one is entitled to such protection under the law, he is said to have a copyright. To the photographer this means that others cannot publish or otherwise reproduce his pictures without first securing his consent. Such a right must be valued very highly. Without it anyone can reproduce a valuable picture without paying for the privilege.

COMMON LAW COPYRIGHT

Every picture produced by the photographer is, in the beginning, protected by what is called common law copyright.[3] Without any copyright notice or registration, the photographer has the right to prevent others from reproducing his pictures. This protection, however, lasts only until the photographer publishes the picture, or authorizes someone else to do so. The moment the picture is published, the common law copyright is lost, and the photographer must be in a position to rely on statutory copyright secured according to the rules laid down in the Copyright Act.

Common law copyright was defined by New York State's highest court in the recent case of *Estate of Ernest Hemingway v. Random House Inc.,* 23 N.Y. 2d 341 (also discussed in the "Right of Privacy" chapter) as follows:

> Common-law copyright is the term applied to an author's proprietary interest in his literary creations before they have been made generally available to the public. It enables the author to exercise control over the first publication of his work or to prevent publication entirely—hence, its other name, the "right of first publication."

Many amateur photographers rely on common law copyright, especially if they have no intention of selling or publishing their pictures, and it is in fact adequate for their purposes, since the common law right is never lost until publication of the photograph. But the lines of common law copyrights are vague: the inclusion of a photograph in an exhibit where others are permitted to "photograph the photograph," or distribution of copies to a limited number of people for a special purpose amounting to "publication" for this purpose can be close questions. The courts have tended, in recent years, to find that such a special purpose "limited publication" did not divest the photographer of his copyright.

For example, in the *Paulsen v. Personality Posters Inc.* case, 299 N.Y.S. 2nd 501, discussed in Chapter 2, the question of common law copyright also arose. The court held that upon the owner's assent to general publication, the common law copyright terminates. Since there was a sharp disagreement as to the purpose for which the picture was delivered to defendant, the court held it could not decide such an issue in advance of the trial. The court said:

> While submission of the work to a particular person, or selected group of persons, for a limited purpose, and without right of diffusion, reproduction, distribution or sale, would be considered a "limited publication" which would not result in loss of the common-law copyright (see *White v. Kimmell* . . .), there is sharp disagreement between the parties herein as to whether the photograph was sent to defendant for a limited purpose or whether, as defendant claims, it was a completely unrestricted and unlimited submission for purposes of general publication, which would have resulted in a loss of any common-law copyright, which plaintiff may have had in the work (see *American Visuals Corp. v. Holland*, . . .). Since such sharp factual dispute on the issue of publication must be resolved at a trial and precludes the granting of the preliminary injunctive relief sought (see *Morrin v. Structural Steel Board of Trade Inc.*, 231 App. Div. 673, 248 N.Y.S. 273), it becomes unnecessary to consider at this juncture whether the moving papers sufficiently establish that plaintiff in fact possessed a common-law copyright in the photograph in issue.

However, a photographer who has a question about whether a contemplated use of a particular photograph is a "publication" or not is following the best and safest course if he obtains a statutory copyright rather than relying on the common law copyright.

Two 1964 decisions by the United States Supreme Court seemed to some lawyers to cast a cloud on the continued validity of common law copyright. One of these cases, *Sears Roebuck & Co. v. Stiffel Co.*[4] involved a pole-lamp created by Stiffel on which it had obtained a design patent. The lamp was copied by the defendant, which sold its copies at a much lower price. In the course of the litigation between the parties, the design patent was declared to be invalid. The Supreme Court said that federal laws had preempted the areas of copyright and patent and that a state could not, under its unfair competition laws, prevent copying of an unpatented or uncopyrighted article. Since the design patent on the lamp was invalid, the Supreme Court held that anyone could freely copy it. We believe, however, and several lower courts have already held[5] that the Supreme Court decisions in the lamp cases[6] do not have any effect on common law copyright, because the Copyright Act specifically says that it shall not "be construed to annul or limit the right of the author or proprietor of an unpublished work . . . to prevent the copying, publication, or use of such unpublished work. . . ."[7] Thus, as far as unpublished works are concerned, federal law has not "preempted" the area—has not made it impossible for state law dealing with common law copyright to be upheld.

Therefore, where statutory copyright is too impractical and costly, common law copyright may still be relied on. But some knowledge of statutory copyright is indeed important and essential to all those photographers who publish or exhibit their work. Let us turn to a consideration of this somewhat complex subject matter.

WHO MAY COPYRIGHT

The owner of the common law copyright is called the copyright *proprietor*. Ordinarily the photographer, since he is the person who "creates" the picture, will be the copyright proprietor. The situation is different, however, when the photographer is hired to make pictures for a customer. Although the photographer in this instance has been held in some jurisdictions to have a restricted ownership in the negatives or plates, it is safe to say that the customer, and not the photographer, is entitled to the copyright.[8] We have already pointed out in a previous chapter that where a photographer takes a picture gratuitously and at his own expense, he owns the negative and photograph outright. Under such circumstances he alone is the copyright proprietor. Who has the right to copyright can, of course, be changed in any particular instance by an agreement between the parties.

HOW TO SECURE STATUTORY COPYRIGHT FOR UNPUBLISHED PHOTOGRAPHS

Copyright may be secured in an unpublished photograph by the deposit in the Copyright Office of one complete copy of the photograph, an application Form J, and a fee of $4. The copy deposited will be retained. Do not send the only copy.

If the work is subsequently published, another registration will be necessary (see the information below concerning published works), along with another fee. If the work is published after registration and the notice of copyright on the copies of the published version contains a year date, it should be the year date of registration of the claim in the unpublished version. If, however, there is new copyrightable matter in the published version, the year date of publication may be used; it may be advisable to use both dates.

The first term of copyright is 28 years as computed (in the case of unpublished photographs) from the date of registration. In the twenty-eighth year an application may be filed to renew the claim to copyright for a second term of 28 years. Many copyright lawyers believe that there should be a single copyright term which would last until 50 years after the death of the creator of the copyrighted work. It now seems possible that the work on a proposed copyright law revision now being done by the Register of Copyrights and his Panel of Experts, Committees of the American Bar Association, and other representatives and members of the Copyright Bar will result in a new copyright law which will incorporate the "life plus 50" copyright term. If this happens, existing copyrights will be extended accordingly. In a letter to *The New York Times,* which appeared on August 2, 1970, the Authors League of America points out that the pending Copyright Revision Bill, which would establish copyright for the author's life plus 50 years, has endured a decade of discussion, and the league urges prompt enactment of this long awaited revision.

SECURING COPYRIGHT FOR PUBLISHED PHOTOGRAPHS

Copyright may be secured in a photograph (in which a claim to copyright was not registered prior to publication) by publication of the photograph with a notice of copyright on each copy consisting of the word "Copyright," the abbreviation "Copr.," or the symbol © accompanied by the name of the copyright owner. The initials, mark, or monogram of the copyright owner may be used with the symbol © in place of the name if the name appears on some accessible portion of the copies. The year date of publication may be included in the notice, though this is not required for photographs (for example, © John Doe 1957). The use of the symbol © with the name of the copyright owner and the year date will secure copyright in many countries outside the United States under the provisions of the Universal Copyright Convention, protection which might not be secured by use of any of the alternative forms of notice. As this is written, the Universal Copyright Convention has 49 adherents, including most of the important countries of the world, with new members being added from time to time as the years go by. If the photographer has any interest at all in securing international protection, that form of notice should obviously be used.

The date of publication is defined as ". . . the earliest date when copies of the first authorized edition were placed on sale, sold or publicly distributed . . ."

Publication without notice or with an inadequate notice results in the loss of the copyright (even if there has been a previous registration). Once lost, it cannot be regained.

After publication with notice of copyright, two complete copies of the best edition should be sent to the Register of Copyrights, Library of Congress, Washington, D. C. With them should go an application on Form J and the registration fee of $4. The Copyright Act says that the registration and deposit of copies should follow publication "promptly," but the courts have tended to define "promptly" in a curious way. In the "Merry-Go-Round case" in 1938, the United States Supreme Court said that registration of a claim to copyright fourteen months after publication was prompt enough.[9] Other cases followed, and it is now the belief of most copyright lawyers that basic copyright protection can be preserved by publication with proper notice, even though there is no registration until the 28th year of the copyright term. However, where there is statutory copyright obtained by publication, the photographer will be unable to sue under the Copyright Act for any infringements until he has registered the photograph and obtained a registration certificate. If the Copyright Office should demand that a published work be registered and deposited (it doesn't do this often), it is necessary to comply within three months, or the copyright will be lost.

It must be obvious at this point that the method set forth in the statute for copyrighting photographs is quite cumbersome for photographers, and too expensive if handled on a print by print basis. Note below some of the methods that have been developed to deal with this problem.

METHODS OF BULK FILING

Various methods have been devised by individual photographers and by the Professional Photographers of America, Inc. to ease the copyright burden for the photographer by registering a number of photographs at one time with a single registration application and one $4.00 fee. The P.P.A. plan (since dropped because of insufficient demand) provided for photographers to assign their literary rights in photographs to the P.P.A., which would make one registration of a number of prints, or of the P.P.A. group of photographs on microfilm. The Copyright Office was willing to accept this bulk filing with a single form and $4.00. While, as stated above, this plan is no longer available, bulk filing is still a good idea and can also be put into use by the individual photographer.

One might, for example, follow the method outlined by Philippe Halsman some years ago. He selects the photographs which he considers valuable and places a copyright notice on them. He then places the pictures to be copyrighted in a group of a dozen or more on the floor, photographs them, and send the print to Washington with the application for registration and one $4.00 filing fee. Or, for a photographer who finds it convenient, a number of photographs can be put on a roll of microfilm, as was sometimes done by the P.P.A.

Another method is to make up any number of photographs into a "book," which should have a collective title and a title page, but need not be elaborately bound (Acco fasteners or the like will do nicely). The book can be published by selling several copies to friends and perhaps persuading one or two libraries to place it on their shelves, or else by having it placed on sale in a local book or camera store. With a copyright notice on the title page, this publication and a subsequent $4.00 registration will give full protection to all the pictures in the book. (As the copyright law stands now, a "book" cannot be registered in the Copyright Office unless it is published. There is a possibility that this will be changed if a new copyright law is passed.) The chief disadvantage of this method is that a number of copies of the "book" will be needed — several for publication purposes, two for the copyright office, and at least one to keep. But the prints in the "book" (if the pictures are otherwise unpublished) need not be of the quality or size of the unpublished originals, the Copyright Office requires deposit of two copies of "the best edition then published," and such a "best edition" can be quite modest.

LIFE OF COPYRIGHT

A statutory copyright has a life of 28 years and may be renewed for a further period of 28 years by sending a form "R" and a $2.00 fee during the 28th year of the original term. If the photographer is alive at the time of renewal, he (or anyone to whom he has previously sold or given his renewal rights) has the right to renew. If he has died, any agreements he may have made to dispose of the renewal right are invalid, and his spouse and children have the right to renew. If the photographer left no widow or children, then the photographer's executor or his next of kin will have the right to renew the copyright. If a new copyright law is passed with the provision that there will be only one term, ending 50 years after the "author's" death, then these complicated renewal provisions will be eliminated.

COMMON LAW COPYRIGHT

We have already pointed out that most amateur photographers will not take the steps necessary to secure a statutory copyright. In most cases, the amateur will not have to worry about his pictures falling into the public domain unless he places them on public exhibition or sells them. If he sends his pictures to a photographic magazine and they are published, a statutory copyright will be secured by the publisher on the entire contents of the magazine including the photographer's picture. Even if the photographer sells the publication only limited reproduction rights, so long as the publisher has authority to copyright the picture in the publisher's name, the publisher's copyright keeps the picture from falling into the public domain, and the photographer still owns whatever rights he did not sell to the publisher.[10] Some authorities believe (and it is common practice) that it is better for the photographer to assign all of his rights to the publisher, then have the publisher assign back, after the picture has been published with the publisher's copyright notice, those rights which the photographer did not agree to part with permanently. This is one way of making it very clear that the publisher did have the right to copyright the picture in its name. If it were shown that the publisher did not have the right to secure copyright in a picture, the copyright notice on the magazine might not protect that picture.

Exhibition of photographs still involves some risk of a court's holding that common law copyright on the exhibited picture is forfeited. However, decisions in the Federal courts over the last ten or fifteen years have set the precedent that the court may not give such broad interpretation to the word "publication" as to deprive a person of his common law copyright in photographs merely because he exhibited them.[11]

It should also be pointed out for the benefit of those who choose to rest upon a common law copyright for pictures which

Page 1

FORM J

CLASS	REGISTRATION NO.
J	
	DO NOT WRITE HERE

Application for Registration of a Claim to Copyright
in a photograph

Instructions: Read the information provided on page 4 before completing the form. Fill in applicable items on all pages. Follow the instructions which accompany each item. In the case of published works the application should give the facts which existed at the date of publication. Pages 1 and 2 should be typewritten or printed with pen and ink. Pages 3 and 4 may be carbon copies. Mail all pages to the Register of Copyrights,

Library of Congress, Washington 25, D. C., together with:

(*a*) If unpublished, one copy of the photograph and the registration fee of $4.

(*b*) If published, two copies of the photograph and the registration fee of $4.

Make your remittance payable to the Register of Copyrights.

1. Copyright Claimant(s) and Address(es): Give the name(s) and address(es) of the copyright owner(s). In the case of published works the name should ordinarily be the same as in the notice of copyright on the copies or, if initials are used in the notice, the name should be the same as appears elsewhere on the copies of the work deposited.

Name _____

Address _____

Name _____

Address _____

2. Title: Give the title of the photograph as it appears on the copies. For purposes of identification each copy deposited should bear a title.

3. Author: The citizenship of the author and information concerning domicile must be given. If an organization is the author and was formed under the laws of the United States, the case of a work made for hire the employer is the author. If the claim is based on new matter (see item 5) give information about the author of the new matter.

(Name of country)

Domiciled in U. S. A. Yes ☐ No ☐ Address _____

4. Date and Place of Publication (for published works only):

(*a*) Give the date (month, day, and year) when copies were first placed on sale, sold, or publicly distributed.

_____

(*b*) Give the name of the country in which the work was first published.

_____

5. Previous Registration or Publication:

If a claim to copyright in any portion of the work was previously registered, or if part of the work was previously published, check the appropriate space (check both if applicable):

☐ Previous registration

☐ Previous publication

and give a brief general statement of the nature of the new matter in this version:

_____

_____

16—68827-3

See next page

have not been sold, that a photographer who seeks the benefit of copyright protection based on publication also takes some risks, and suffers some disadvantages. If his copyright notice, at the time of publication, is not correct, or if it is omitted from some of the published copies, the copyright may be forever lost. Also, if he does not remember to renew his copyright during the 28th year, it will expire. A common law copyright, unlike a statutory copyright, can go on forever under the present law — and the 28-year first term of copyright does not begin until there has been either registration or publication with proper copyright notice. As pointed out before, publication *without proper copyright notice* will cause the loss of all literary property rights in the photograph and neither common law nor statutory copyright will ever be available for that picture thereafter.

ASSIGNMENT OF COPYRIGHT

A photographer may assign his copyright on a photograph. The purchaser (or other assignee) should send the assignment to the Copyright Office for recording within three months, since the law protects him against subsequent assignments by the photographer of the same picture to others. The fee for recording the assignment is $3.00. Between the photographer and the assignee, however, the assignment is valid even if it is not recorded. An assignment of statutory copyright must be in writing to be valid; an assignment of common law copyright can be valid even if oral, although it is better to have it in writing. An assignment of common law copyright need not be recorded. An assignment of copyright during the first 28-year term does not convey any rights for the renewal term, unless it is clear from the language of the assignment that the photographer intended to assign renewal rights.

COPYRIGHT INFRINGEMENT

Everyone knows that a copyrighted photograph may not be copied or reproduced without the copyright owner's permission.

A violation of this rule subjects the infringer to suit for damages for copyright infringement.

There is a vast difference, however, between copying a picture and photographing the same subject matter. A copyright on a picture does not prevent another person from independently photographing a similar subject. Another photographer may even take a picture of a subject in exactly the same manner as did the first photographer as long as the second picture has been made independently of the first. The question is, how do you determine whether a picture was taken independently or with the idea of duplicating the previous picture? The latter is a violation of law, the former is not. The following statement of facts, taken from a federal case which was settled before trial a few years ago, illustrates the problem. The picture of a model taken by the plaintiff appeared on the cover of a magazine. The plaintiff photographer charged in his complaint that although a picture of the same model taken by the defendant was not an exact copy, the model was photographed by the defendant with the plaintiff's picture before him. The defendant, it was charged, had posed the model in the same position, wearing the same costume, with the identical color scheme as that in the plaintiff's photo. It was further charged that the defendant's intention was to copy the plaintiff's picture with slight differences for the purpose of making it possible to appropriate the essential features of the picture, thus evading the copyright laws. Had a court found that this was indeed what the defendant had done, we believe that a judgment in favor of the plaintiff for copyright infringement would have been correct. Copying a copyrighted photograph, by whatever method, is a copyright infringement.

The leading case on this subject was decided in 1914 and is known as the Grace of Youth Case.[12] A photographer was held guilty of infringement of a photograph he had taken of a girl model. The photographer sold all his rights, including the copyright to the picture. Two years later he photographed the same model with the idea of obtaining a similar picture of her without being bound by the copyright restrictions on the first picture, which now belonged to someone else. The court would not permit such action and expressed itself most vigorously on the subject. The court said:

> It seems to us, however, that we have no such new photograph of the same model. The identity of the artist and the many close identities of pose, light and shade, etc., indicate very strongly that the first picture was used to produce the second. Whether the model in the second case was posed, and light and shade, etc., arranged with a copy of the first photograph physically present before the artist's eyes, or whether his mental reproduction of the exact combination he had already once effected was so clear and vivid that he did not need the physical reproduction of it, seems to us immaterial. The one thing, viz., the exercise of artistic talent, which made the first photographic picture a subject of copyright, has been used not to produce another picture, but to duplicate the original . . .
>
> The eye of an artist or a connoisseur will, no doubt, find. differences between these two photographs. The backgrounds are not identical, the model in one case is sedate, in the other smiling; moreover the young woman was two years older when the later photograph was taken, and some slight changes in the contours of her figure are discoverable. But the identities are much greater than the differences, and it seems to us that the artist was careful to introduce only enough differences to argue about, while undertaking to make what would seem to be a copy to the ordinary purchaser who did not have both photographs before him at the same time. In this undertaking we think he succeeded.

As a result of this case and others which have followed, the law appears to be well settled on the point that one cannot evade the copyright statute by the simple ruse of taking a separate picture of the same subject and introducing just enough differences to argue about.

However, this should not deter photographers from going about their usual business and taking photographs of any and all subjects, animate and inanimate, just because others may have previously photographed them and copyrighted such pictures. The question is one of the exercise of artistic talent. If a photographer exercises his own in taking a picture he is on safe ground. If he takes advantage of the artistic talent of another — if he copies — his action is open to question.

Copying can, of course, take place in other ways. One of the interesting cases on this subject involved a copyrighted photograph of a tiger. A magazine made a drawing from the photograph and published it. An English court held this to be an infringement.[13] Thus, a copy need not be in the same medium as the original in order to constitute an infringement.

In this connection the photographer should note that when he photographs a work of art in a museum or elsewhere (such as a painting or statue he might see in a store window), he may run afoul of the copyright laws if the work of art is protected by either common law or statutory copyright. As a practical matter (other than securing permission to take the picture from the museum or the person or firm in possession of the work of art), making such pictures for one's own enjoyment seldom creates a problem. It is the sale of reproduction rights to such a photo that can cause trouble. Technically, the painter, sculptor or other copyright owner could and should object to the reproduction itself.

CHAPTER VII

Libel By Photograph

LIBEL BY PHOTOGRAPH is a problem that is closer to both amateur and professional photographers than they generally realize. We were recently told by a photographer that a picture cannot possibly be libelous (at least if it has not been doctored), since a picture tells the truth and the truth cannot be a libel. He was wrong on the first count, and not entirely right on the second.

First, we all know that pictures do not always tell the truth. Optical illusions are sometimes created by the camera just as they are by the human eye — a point that was made quite clear by a very interesting case in the Federal Courts some years ago.

In that case[1] the plaintiff was a widely known gentleman steeple-chaser whose picture was used in connection with an endorsement for Camel cigarettes. Plaintiff had posed for the picture in question willingly and had been paid for his testimonial. He did not, however, see the photograph before it was actually used. By a quirk of lighting, the picture showed the horesman with his hand under the pommel, and the side girth fell loosely in such a way that it seemed to be attached to the plaintiff's middle rather than to the saddle. Looked at in this way the photograph became, in the words of the court, "grotesque, monstrous and obscene;" and the legend carried on a second photograph of plaintiff in the same advertisement which said, "Get a Lift with a Camel" reinforced the ribald interpretation.

The court recognized that an optical illusion had been created and that the photograph carried "its correction on its face as much as though it were a verbal utterance which expressly declared it was false . . ." Nevertheless, the court said, the picture exposed the plaintiff to overwhelming ridicule. It made of the plaintiff a preposterous, ridiculous spectacle and the obvious mistake only added to the amusement. The court added that "had such a picture been deliberately reproduced, surely every right-minded person would agree that he would have had a genuine grievance; and the effect is the same whether it is deliberate or not."

As to the plaintiff's having consented to the use of the photographs for which he posed for an advertisement, the court ruled that this was not a consent to the use of an offending photograph. The plaintiff had no reason to anticipate that the lens would so distort his appearance. The Court would not fix upon the plaintiff the responsibility for whatever the camera might turn out, as long as he did not see and approve the picture before publication.

While the case of the steeple-chaser may seem a bit unusual as to its facts, the Court's decision in the case rests on certain basic elements in the law of libel, which all photographers should understand.

A FEW BASIC PRINCIPLES

A libel, as it is defined in the law dictionaries, is that which is written or printed, and published, and which injures the reputation of another by bringing him into ridicule, hatred or contempt. While truth is generally regarded as an absolute defense to libel, there are some jurisdictions which hold that even truth is not a defense if the libel was malicious.[2] Here are some typical examples of statements that have been held libelous by the courts. It is a libel to say that a man is insane, or that he has an infectious disease, or that he is illegitimate, or that he is guilty of a crime, or that a woman was served with a summons in her bathtub.

To avoid any possible confusion, we should also point out that there are instances other than where truth is relied on as a defense where the publisher of a false and defamatory statement has the privilege to publish. For example, Congressmen have an absolute privilege in a speech or debate in either House of Congress; and newspapers may report statements made in legislative or judicial proceedings, provided the report is fair and accurate. There are other privileges but they are not important to our discussion at this time. Note also that good intentions and innocent mistakes are not defenses to an action of libel, although it is possible that accidental libel may be considered by the jury in awarding damages.[3]

Applying the basic principles of libel to photography, the Courts have rightfully said that a man may be held up as an object of ridicule, contempt or hatred by means of a picture, just as he can by words.

NECESSITY OF PUBLICATION

You may have noted in the definition of the term "libel" that a publication is required. This does not mean that only pictures which appear in magazines or newspapers can be libelous. The term "publication" is far broader than this and includes all types of display. Thus, if a photographer places one of his prints in a showcase in front of his studio or shows the picture to people other than the subject, he has "published" that print for the purposes of the law of libel. Mere possession of a print is not publication. The distinction is important.

CAPTIONS ON PHOTOGRAPHS

One particular area in which photographs must exercise caution involves the captions placed on pictures, for a perfectly harmless photograph can be made libelous by an improper caption.

The photograph of the steeplechaser did not require a caption to make it libelous. But here are some cases where captions caused the trouble. In one instance the words "Fatty Arbuckle's Lady Love" were printed below the picture of the plaintiff. The publication was held libelous,[4] for the plaintiff was a married woman and the combination of picture and caption held her up to disgrace. The Court said that the combination imputed an illicit relationship between the plaintiff and the obese comedian. The same result was reached where a picture of the one-time wrestling champion Zbyszko was captioned "Stanislaus Zbyszko, Wrestler, Not Fundamentally Different From the Gorilla in Physique." The wrestler's picture was placed next to that of a gorilla.[5]

Another interesting example of this problem occurred several years ago when a mid-Western newspaper published the photographs of four school boys under the banner headline: "Slain School Girl Vanished with Someone in Cadillac." Immediately below these pictures, in small type, was the further explanation: "These four acquaintances of murdered Patricia Birmingham are co-operating with police in seeking clues that may lead to the girl's slayer." This was followed by the names and addresses of the boys.

Five or six lines below the pictures, in type five to six times larger than that in the line immediately below the photographs, was a two column sub-head: "Four Youths Held; 60 to 70 Friends Face Grilling." The boys brought an action for libel and the court held[6] that it was a question of fact whether the photographs, captions and heads combined were capable of conveying the meaning that the four boys were the boys held on suspicion of murder. In other words, the question was one for the jury.

Such cases demonstrate the absolute necessity of caution in placing captions on photographs. The photographer *must* ask himself — could picture and caption together reasonably be construed as holding someone up to ridicule? A seemingly innocent caption may often be offensive. For example, one publisher was recently threatened with a lawsuit for publishing a photograph of two women standing close together, one of whom was lighting a cigaret. The other woman was of substantial proportions and appeared to be shielding her friend from the wind. The photographer used the caption "Windbreaker" on the photograph. While the threatened litigation was avoided, such problems need not arise if a little thought is given to the problem in advance.

PICTURES ACCOMPANYING LIBELOUS ARTICLES

Most libel cases involving photographs arise, however, where the gist of the libel involves an accompanying article or story — not just a caption. For example, a New York newspaper published an article about dishonesty at auctions. Accompanying the article was an untitled picture of the plaintiff who was not even an auctioneer. Obviously, an improper inference concerning the plaintiff could be drawn from picture and article together, and the court said it was libel.[7]

In another case[8] a newspaper published an article about a dancer. To illustrate it they used a picture of the dancer which she had posed for in the nude. The court said this was libel, for picture and story were not sufficiently related.

An interesting question arises in the case of a group picture, such as a picture of a crowd, when the picture itself is not defamatory but the use made of it is, as when it accompanies an article or news item of a libelous nature. Can a person shown in such a picture sue for libel? In *St. John v. New York Times* (New York Supreme Court, N.Y. Law Journal, August 10, 1966), the article portrayed a cross section of personalities who study bound volumes of the *Morning Telegraph* (a race horse publication) in the New York Public Library Annex. One of the persons shown in the picture sued for libel and violation of right of privacy, claiming that the article was an exposé of persons who surreptitiously, without their bosses' knowledge, waste their time in the public library charting race horses and that it described the persons as "drifters" of "seedy" appearance. The court dismissed the complaint, holding that none of the libelous statements were directed at the plaintiff nor was he in any way identified in the picture, saying:

> . . . "In addition, the law is clear that where a defamatory publication affects a class of persons, no member of that class can maintain an action therefor unless it is applicable to every member of the class or is specifically applicable to a particular member" (53 Corpus Juris Secundum, Sec. 11, p. 55). This is graphically illustrated in the case of *Cohn v. Brecker,* 20 Misc. 2d 329, where the court in dismissing the complaint stated:

"Here the words refer to one not specified of a group of persons. Whereas it is essential that the 'defamatory words must refer to some ascertained or ascertainable person and that person must be the plaintiff . . . So, if the words reflect impartially on either A. or B., or on some of a certain number or class, and there is nothing to show which one was meant, no one can sue.' *Feely v. Vitagraph Co.,* 184 App. Div. 527, 528" (p. 330)

In *Vogel v. Hearst Corporation,* 116 N.Y.S. 2d 905, the picture of plaintiff, a young girl not otherwise identified, appeared accompanying a magazine article ascribed by her to be libelous. The complaint there was dismissed on the ground that the words of the article reflected on no ascertainable person. To the same effect see *Hays v. American Defense Society,* 252 N.Y. 266, 274-6; *Julian v. American Business Consultants Inc.,* 2 N.Y. 2d 1, 14-18. In the case at bar, any reading of the article in no way discloses the descriptive language which plaintiff finds objectionable as ascertainably aimed at him, either individually or by virtue of any reference to all of the members of the group. The article in general, portrays a cross-section of personalities who study bound volumes of the Morning Telegraph Newspaper in the New York Public Library Annex. Plaintiff in nowise is referred to personally or accused of surreptitiously charting horses on business time or of even being seedy or without employment. The article simply refers to "some," "others," "at least one man," "most," and "the hard core" and describes a wide variety of types and personalities. It speaks of "bright eyes, rheumy eyes, eyes blinking into focus behind ashtray-thick spectacles and of striding, shuffling, limping" (Complaint, Paragraph Ten). Manifestly, no one person has all of these characteristics. Nor does plaintiff's name appear anywhere in the article or picture nor is he in any way described in the article. The only identification alleged by him is that it is in the photograph, but it must be noted that he has not seen fit to include it as part of his complaint. Accordingly, it cannot be said that any defamatory publication "of and concerning" the plaintiff has been made in the complaint.

MISTAKEN IDENTITY MAY BE LIBEL

Suppose a newspaper published a story about Mr. John Jones, who has been accused of committing a crime. There is more than one John Jones in the city, however, and the newspaper published a picture of the wrong Mr. Jones with its story. The result is libel. Similarly, in a case where a testimonial for a particular brand of whiskey was signed by one person and the publication used a picture

of the wrong person with it, the court held that the plaintiff's grievance should be submitted to a jury.[9]

PICTURES OF A PLACE

Improper use of a photograph to illustrate a story can even
extend to pictures of buildings. Where, for example, an article on
illegal banking procedures was dressed up with the photograph of
an innocent banking institution, the bank won a jury verdict for
libel.[10]

RETOUCHING PHOTOS

One other area which requires comment involves retouching
of photographs. Although this problem has already been covered
in the section on model releases in Chapter 2, it is worth noting
again that a changed photograph may be objectionable to the subject even though the original was not.

CONCLUSION

Finally, let it be noted once again that most cases arising
under the law of libel involve questions of fact for the jury to decide.
It is wise, therefore, for the photographer to examine carefully
those pictures which he intends to publish, particularly the captions,
and to avoid those which might seem clever but could possibly hold
the subject up to ridicule.

CHAPTER VIII

Photographs As Evidence

AT THE OUTSET it should be noted that many books on the subject
of evidence have been written. In these the subject of photographs
as evidence has been treated in far greater detail than it is possible
to do in the space allocated for this subject in this book. What
follows is a brief discussion of the subject designed to give photographers a general idea of the use of photographs in a courtroom.

In general, photographs, when shown to be a correct resem-
blance of the person or thing represented, are competent as evidence. The highest court in New York[1] has commented as follows
on photographs as evidence:

> We do not fail to notice, and we may notice judicially, that all
> civilized communities rely upon photographic pictures for taking
> and presenting resemblances of persons and animals, of scenery and
> all natural objects, of buildings and other artificial objects. It is of
> frequent occurrence, that fugitives from justice are arrested on the
> identification given by them. "The Rogues' Gallery" is the practical
> judgment of the executive officers of the law on their efficiency and
> accuracy. They are signs of the things taken.
>
> A portrait or a miniature taken by a skilled artist, and proven
> to be an accurate likeness, would be received on a question of the
> identity or the appearance of a person not producible in court. Photo-
> graphic pictures do not differ in kind of proof from the pictures of
> a painter. They are the products of natural laws and a scientific
> process. It is true that in the hands of a bungler, who is not apt in
> the use of the process, the result may not be satisfactory. Somewhat
> [sic] depends for exact likeness upon the nice adjustment of ma-
> chinery, upon atmospheric conditions, upon the position of the sub-
> ject, the intensity of the light, the length of the sitting. It is the skill

of the operator that takes care of these, as it is the skill of the artist that makes correct drawing of features, and nice mingling of tints, for the portrait. Most of evidence is but the signs of things. . . .

So the signs of the portrait and the photograph, if authenticated by other testimony, may give truthful representations. When shown by such testimony to be correct resemblances of a person, we see not why they may not be shown to the triers of the facts, not as conclusive, but as aids in determining the matter in issue, still being open like proofs of identity or similar matter, to rebuttal or doubt.

PHYSICAL APPEARANCE AND IDENTITY

In actions for personal injuries courts have permitted photographic evidence as to the appearance of persons. In one case a photograph of the injured person showing the manner in which his limbs had been contracted was admitted into evidence after a physician certified that it was taken in his presence and correctly represented the condition of his limbs. It should, of course, be pointed out that a proper foundation must first be laid for the introduction of the photograph, consisting of testimony that the picture is a true representation of the condition of the person as of a particular time. The court in this case said:

> During the trial, the plaintiff's counsel offered in evidence a photograph of the plaintiff showing the manner in which his limbs were contracted. This was permitted by the court under the objection of the defendant. Before it was done, however, one of the doctors testified that the photograph was taken in his presence and that it correctly represented the condition of the limbs. The only materiality of this evidence was to show the manner in which the limbs of the plaintiff were contracted. In this regard, the testimony of the physician is that it was a correct representation of them. This made it competent as a map or diagram.[2]

Of course, there are very definite limitations on the use of photographs as evidence. If it can be shown that the photograph does not represent the true condition of the subject of the case or that it is misleading, it will not be received in evidence. For example, where the issue in the case was the appearance of a young girl at the time of an accident, a photograph taken one year before the accident was held on appeal to have been improperly received in evidence. The Appellate Court said:

> A photograph of the plaintiff, taken a year before the employment, in the dress worn by her when she received her first Holy Communion, was admitted in evidence over the defendant's objection, upon testimony to the effect that it correctly represented the plaintiff's appearance at the time of the accident; that she was about the size indicated by the photograph when employed; and that the picture looked as she did when she was employed. We all know that dress alone makes a great deal of difference in the apparent age of a person. The combination of dress and a photograph would be doubly deceptive. When employed, the plaintiff was six months below the age fixed by the statute. A photograph taken a year before, dressed as she was, with veil and flowers on her head, short white dress, white slippers and stockings, was no evidence of her appearance as to age when employed. The prejudicial character of the photograph is manifest. It could have served no possible purpose except to mislead, and its misleading character is the more manifest when we consider that the question at issue was the apparent age of a girl at a rapidly developing period of her life.[3]

In an action for death caused by negligence, the admission of a photo of the decedent and his children taken about six months before his death was also held[4] erroneous as calculated to arouse the sympathy of the jury. And in an action for personal injuries to a vaudeville dancer who was struck by an automobile, an Appellate Court reversed a decision of the Trial Court to permit the introduction of a motion picture on the following grounds: the film, showing the plaintiff dancing *prior* to the accident despite an artificial leg (which did not prevent him from carrying on his work) was inadmissible since it made a farce of the trial. The Court said:

> Aside from the fact that moving pictures present a fertile field for exaggeration of any emotion or action, and the absence of evidence as to how this particular motion picture was prepared, we think the picture admitted in evidence brought before the jury irrelevant matter, hearsay and incompetent evidence and tended to make a farce of the trial.[5]

In another case it was held that in actions for personal injuries capable of verbal description, it was error to admit a photograph of the injuries into evidence.[6]

Thus it can be seen from the foregoing that pictures are admissible only under certain conditions and where a proper foundation for them has first been laid.

CONDITION OF PREMISES

The rules governing admission of photos to show the physical condition and identity of persons apply to photographs depicting the condition of premises. Thus it has been held[7] that in an action for damages to premises, a photograph of the premises at the time of the accident is admissible. And in another case, a high court in New York stated the rule:

> If a fair representation of the premises, it was admissible as an aid in the investigation, as much so as a map or other diagram and served in a like manner to explain or illustrate and apply testimony.... Of course, its value, like the value of other evidence, depends upon its accuracy.

MOVING PICTURES

There have been numerous cases involving the propriety of the admission of moving pictures in evidence. A court[8] held that if the pictures are sensational only and unnecessary, particularly where the facts may be described or evidence submitted in another form, they should be excluded. The court said:

> The admissibility in evidence of moving pictures has been before the courts of the state several times and there appears to be very decided and divergent views with reference to their admission in evidence.... In no case should they be admitted unless a proper foundation has been laid therefor. In most cases the question should be left largely to the discretion of the trial judge. If a trial is to be unduly delayed by exhibiting moving pictures, the court may very properly refuse to permit such a delay. If moving pictures are sensational only and unnecessary, the court should refuse to permit such evidence, particularly where the facts may be described or the evidence submitted in another form and thus avoid the delay and difficulty which will result from their introduction. If their use is solely for the purpose of advertisement or in an effort to obtain publicity, they should not be allowed in evidence. Several cases have been cited where evidence of moving pictures has been properly rejected. In these cases the purpose was shown to be merely sensational. Where there is no need of such pictures, as in several of the cases adverted to, the trial court is within its right in rejecting such testimony.

CHAPTER IX

Photography—
Business, Art or Profession?

BUSINESS, ART OR PROFESSION — what is photography? And what difference does it make? The question can arise in various ways and is one of particular importance legally to the professional photographer. Here is why.

A photographer opens a studio in a community which has an unincorporated business tax. The law exempts persons engaged in a profession. Is the photographer exempt? A license tax is imposed on those engaged in a mechanical pursuit. Is the photographer included? A law exempts implements of trade from levy by creditors. Is a lens an implement of trade? Regulations are imposed on manufacturing businesses. Do they apply to a particular photographic business? These are but a few of the many instances in which the courts have been called upon to define the status of photography.

The courts have called photography everything from a trade to a science. There has been no unanimity of opinion on the subject, but the courts have generally said that the photographer should be regarded as an artist.

Back in 1890 a Louisiana court had to decide whether a photographer should pay a certain tax. The state constitution exempted all persons engaged in mechanical pursuits from the payment of the tax, and the photographer claimed the exemption. In denying the exemption, the court said that, as distinguished from a mechanical pursuit, photography is a science, or at least a liberal art, in which the desired results could not be accomplished by the spontaneous action of the apparatus employed, but required the agency of a photographer

> who, to operate successfully, must necessarily be, and prove himself, a most intelligent artist, calling into activity not only his hands, senses and body, but also and chiefly, in order to control them, his scientific aptitudes and superintending mind. . . . The science or art which he practices is not a useful or mechanical science or art, (one in which the hands and body are more concerned than the brain) but at least, a liberal or polite art — scientific to a quite considerable extent, the practice of which is made efficient and valuable only by knowledge and skill, as the result of some science, observation, combination and experimentation not readily acquired.[1]

A Tennessee court took a similar view in 1883, when it ruled that a photographer is not a mechanic within the meaning of a statute which exempted mechanics' tools from seizure to satisfy a judgment. The Court said:

> The photographer is an artist, not an artisan, who takes impressions or likenesses of things and persons on prepared plates or surfaces. He is no more a mechanic than the painter who, by means of his pigments, covers his canvas with the glaring images of natural objects.[2]

Over thirty years ago a British court decided that a photographer is not a professional man. The photographer offered proof to show that his photographs were different from those of the average photographer. The court recognized him as an outstanding photographer but refused to elevate him to the status of a professional man, saying:

> It was true that the appellant's work differed from that of an ordinary photographer. He had gone very much beyond the work of the ordinary trade photographer, but he did not, as it appeared to him [his Lordship] do anything in law beyond what an ordinary photographer did.[3]

Of course, the decision of the British court assumes that there can be no question that an ordinary photographer is not a professional man, and the argument advanced for the photographer in question was that he was an extraordinary photographer. Any distinction between ordinary and extraordinary photographers seems baseless, for if photography itself is a profession, anyone practicing it is a professional man.

The New York courts have not found it necessary to classify photography specifically, but a New York court did say in 1931 that a photographic business could not be classified as manufacturing.[4]

A business tax is imposed in New York on unincorporated business. Persons engaged in a profession are exempt. Photographers have not yet tested whether this law applies to them, but if they should, here is the test of a profession, established by the highest court in the state, which they will have to meet. A profession requires "knowledge of an advanced type in a given field of science or learning gained by a prolonged course of specialized instruction and study."[5]

LICENSING STATUTES

Further clues as to the status of photography in the eyes of the law are found in decisions involving the right of states to require licenses from those desiring to engage in photography. In most states where such legislation was enacted the courts have invalidated the statutes as being an unwarranted interference with the right of an individual to engage in a lawful occupation which does not so affect the public welfare as to warrant state regulation. An Arizona Court in 1941 held:

> The *business or profession* of taking photographs of people, animals and things does not need regulation. It is one of the innocent, usual occupations in which everybody who wishes may indulge as a pastime or a hobby or a vocation, without harm or injury to anybody, or to the general welfare, or the public health and morals, or the peace, safety and comfort of the people. It needs no policing.[6]

In 1935 a photographer was convicted in a Hawaiian Court of practicing without a license. The conviction was over-ruled on appeal. The Appellate Court said:

> More specifically the question is, was it within the constitutional power of the legislature to exclude from the practice of photography

for profit all persons who had not complied with the provisions of the Act? The answer to this inquiry depends on the nature of photography — whether as an occupation it is innocent and innocuous or whether it is infected with some quality that might render it dangerous to the morals, the health, the comfort or welfare of those who constitute the public. If the latter is true it is within the police power of the legislature to place upon it the regulations and restrictions contained in the Act. If, on the other hand, the practice of photography is harmless and without detriment to the public welfare, it was beyond the power of the legislature to restrict it to those having a certificate of proficiency.[7]

The Court concluded that the act requiring a license for the practice of photography "is an unconstitutional encroachment upon the liberty of the citizen to choose and pursue an innocent occupation."

In 1938 a Tennessee Court, in over-ruling similar legislation said:

We find it difficult to perceive just how the licensing of photographers and regulation of the taking and finishing of pictures ... has any real tendency to protect the public health or the public morals.[8]

A Georgia court struck down similar legislation,[9] and in 1955 the Montana Supreme Court struck down the Photographic Examiners Act which required persons desiring to engage in portrait, commercial work or photo finishing to procure a license. The Act provided that those engaged in the practice of photography, when it took effect, should be granted a license upon application, but that others must give satisfactory evidence as to competency and fitness to practice photography based on technical knowledge and business integrity. The Court said that the only basis for the Act was to create a monopoly for those persons fortunate enough to be included within the formula of the Act prior to the date it became effective and that the Act was not in the interest of the general welfare. It also condemned the law on the ground that it gave the examining board unlimited authority to choose who was qualified as a photographer. Also in 1955, the Nevada State Assembly refused to act on a proposed law for licensing photographers.

The only discordant judicial note on the licensing question appears to have been sounded in a decision of the North Carolina Courts. It was there decided, by a three-to-two decision, that a photography licensing act was constitutional. However, the dissenting judge in that case said:

> I am therefore unable to conceive how the practice of photography has such a rational and substantial relationship to social needs or to public health, safety and good morals as to make it a subject of legislation under the police power of the state. . . . The regulation of business and professions, through administrative licensing, has heretofore been limited to those professions having a direct and positive relation to the health, safety or morals of the community. The trade of photography bears no general resemblance to any of the professions indicated. . . . While photography requires some skill, it is the same type of skill required by other trades and vocations.[10]

While this statement is in a dissenting opinion and does not represent the view of the majority of the North Carolina court, it seems to be the view of the great majority of the courts in the United States. In other words, the courts have generally freed photography from the shackles of the police power of the states, but at the same time have refused to elevate it to the legal status of a profession.

Photography has made important progress since some of the cases referred to were decided. A vocational guidance pamphlet issued by the Rochester Institute of Technology in 1950 indicates how specialized photography as we know it today has become. There it is noted that many branches exist in the field, such as advertising photography, aerial photography, commercial photography, documentary photography, industrial and scientific photography, motion picture photography, museum photography and photo journalism. Furthermore, a number of colleges and universities have seen fit to accord to photography the status of an art or science by giving courses leading to degrees with majors in photography.* However, these are not legally required courses as a prerequisite to engaging in the practice of photography and anyone is permitted to earn his living at photography in most states. As long as this situation exists, photography cannot meet the legal test

---

*Rochester Institute of Technology (Assoc. in Applied Science); Ohio University (Bachelor of Fine Arts. Major in Photography); University of Houston (Bachelor of Arts, Science or Fine Arts. Major in Photography); University of Southern California (Bachelor of Arts. Major in Cinema); Santa Monica City College

of a profession as laid down by the New York courts, namely, requiring knowledge of an advanced type in a given field of science or learning gained by a prolonged course of specialized instruction and study.

However, photography has not fared too badly in the courts. The weight of authority is in favor of regarding a photographer as an artist. The courts have almost uniformly come to the rescue of photography whenever state regulatory control has been attempted and, except for a few states, licenses are not required in order to engage in professional photography. The courts have stamped photography as an innocent occupation or vocation which may be engaged in without harm or injury to anybody or to the general welfare. The inability of the courts to find a few magic words that will pin a definite label on photography has obviously not prevented this sometime hobby-business-art-profession from flourishing over the years.

More important than the label is the vast area of the rights and obligations of the photographer, both amateur and professional. Right of privacy, restrictions on the taking of photographs, libel, ownership of photographs, copyrights — these and still other areas of law affect everyone who snaps a shutter.

(Associate in Applied Science); Institute of Design, Illinois Institute of Technology (Bachelor of Science in Photography); Maryland State College (Bachelor of Science in Industrial Education or in Mechanical Arts. Major in Photography); Oklahoma Baptist University (Bachelor of Science. Major in Photography).

***LICENSING REQUIREMENTS
FOR PHOTOGRAPHERS IN 50 STATES**

State	No Licensing Provision	Licensing for Fee Only
Alabama		X (a)
Alaska	X	
Arizona	X (b)	
Arkansas		X (f)
California	X	
Colorado	X	
Connecticut	X	
Delaware		X (a)
Florida		X (d)
Georgia	X (e)	
Hawaii	X	
Idaho	X (j)	
Illinois	X	
Indiana	X	
Iowa	X	
Kansas	X (f)	
Kentucky	X	
Louisiana		X
Maine		X (c)
Maryland	X (k)	
Massachusetts	X	
Michigan	X	
Minnesota	X	
Mississippi	X (d)	
Missouri	X (f)	
Montana	X	
Nebraska	X	
Nevada	X	
New Hampshire	X	
New Jersey	X (f)	
New Mexico		X
New York	X	
North Carolina		X (a)
North Dakota	X	
Ohio	X (g)	
Oklahoma	X (f)	
Oregon	X (f)	
Pennsylvania	X (f)	
Rhode Island	X	
South Carolina	X (f)	
South Dakota	X	

Tennessee	X (h)	
Texas	X	
Utah	X (f)	
Vermont		X (c)
Virginia		X (i)
Washington	X (h)	
West Virginia	X (j)	
Wisconsin	X	
Wyoming	X (g)	

*In 1964 a review was made of the licensing provisions of each of the 50 states. In most cases the information set forth concerning licensing requirements was derived from the text of individual statutes. In others, the authors have relied upon communications from the Secretary of State.

Notes on chart of Licensing Statutes:

(a) Statute so worded as to apply to professional photographers only.

(b) Act of 1935 was declared unconstitutional by the Arizona Supreme Court.

(c) Applies only to itinerant photographers.

(d) License must be obtained from Tax Collector of County where photographer does business.

(e) 1937 Statute set up a State Board of Photographic Examiners but was declared unconstitutional. Bramley v. State, (1939) 187 Ga. 826, 2 S.E. (2nd) 647.

(f) Although no State License is required, Statutes provide that cities, or some classes of cities, shall have the power to pass ordinances requiring license for regulation or revenue and inquiry should be made with local authorities.

(g) Bill introduced in 1940 failed to pass.

(h) Although no license is required, photographers, except newspaper photographers, are specifically taxed for doing business.

(i) Virginia also has Statute regulating practice of photography. See act of 1938, 544.

(j) Although no license is required, photographers who sell merchandise, such as picture frames, must obtain a store license.

(k) Although no State license is required, Baltimore City requires a license for persons engaged in the business of taking photographs on the streets or sidewalks.

CHAPTER X

Questions and Answers

FURTHER DETAILS ON many of the points of law considered in the previous chapters are explained in the answers to the questions which follow. These questions are typical of the ones which have been addressed to us as columnists for *Popular Photography* magazine and cover the subjects which most frequently concern the amateur photographer in particular.

QUESTION

Can pictures of accidents on a state thruway be taken without obtaining a special permit?

ANSWER

Pictures may be taken on a state thruway or any other highway whether it is a toll road or not. No permit is necessary.

QUESTION

Can I take pictures in "public" places? Can the management of a railroad station, library, department store or theatre prevent a camera from being brought in or being used for the purpose of taking candid pictures of the crowds?

ANSWER

Pictures can generally be taken in public places. However, libraries, museums, theatres, etc., do have the right to prohibit cameras from being used on the premises or to make whatever restrictions they wish to impose on the taking of pictures. Note that the right to take a picture is not the same as the right to use it, however. Persons who have their pictures taken in public or elsewhere may have a claim for invasion of privacy if the use made of the picture can be classified as advertising or for trade purposes.

QUESTION

I plan to go to Europe this year and will want to photograph as much local color as possible. In snapping candids of people in their own surroundings the element of spontaneity is often lost when the subject is approached to ask permission to photograph them before taking the picture. Is it advisable to take a candid photo without the subject's permission?

ANSWER

It can generally be said that it is not necessary to obtain someone's consent just to take his picture. You must remember that the reason for getting a release or written consent is to permit you to use or publish the picture for advertising or trade purposes. As long as the use which you make of a photograph taken gratuitously is not for advertising or trade purposes and is not libelous in nature, you will generally have no problem.

QUESTION

I would like to take pictures of photographs which I have seen in your magazine. Do I have to ask for permission from the publisher?

ANSWER

Under our copyright laws it would be incumbent upon you, before copying any pictures from magazines or other sources, to find out whether they are copyrighted, for the copyright owner of a picture is the only one who has the right to reproduce it. If the magazine carries a copyright notice, you should obtain permission of the copyright owner before making copies. If you are just making the copies for your own amusement or for educational purposes, there is usually no difficulty in obtaining the necessary consent.

QUESTION

Is it necessary for me to have a model release to sell a picture of a car, truck or farm machinery to a magazine or company for illustrations or advertising?

ANSWER

It is generally believed that you may sell photographs (which you own) of automobiles or farm machinery without obtaining a release from the owner of the particular piece of equipment since the right of privacy protects persons, but not property. The authors know of several lawsuits, however, where the owner of a home or other property claimed that property rights were violated when a photographer took a picture of the home and sold it for an advertising illustration, but these cases were settled before trial. The authors do not know of any case which has decided this question one way or the other, though there have been cases involving photos of property where a decision was based on who owned the photograph and on whether a libel had been committed on the owner of the property. A picture of a reputable bank accompanying an article on crooked banking, for example, was held to be a libel on the bank.

QUESTION

I am an amateur photographer and have talked to one of my friends who is a surgeon about taking a picture of an operation he will perform in the hospital. Will I need a release to publish the picture?

ANSWER

There have been many court decisions in which the use of a photograph of a person undergoing medical treatment was held an invasion of the right of privacy. Technically, the use of such pictures to illustrate articles on medicine should not constitute an invasion of privacy when the use of the picture does not violate one's sense of decency, and some courts have so ruled. Since people are more likely to be sensitive about such pictures it is really important to get consent, and the consent should be both broad and specific.

It is also clear that the consent of a patient to medical or surgical treatment is not tantamount to a consent to take pictures of him in treatment.

QUESTION

I took a picture of a motel for a booklet put out by a local club. A few months later an advertising salesman for the local newspaper asked me for a print of this picture. I quoted him a price for it and he replied, "Why should I pay for a reprint? I will just cut the photograph out of the booklet and make another picture." Does he have a right to do this?

ANSWER

If the picture which you took was properly copyrighted, no one can reproduce your picture without violating the copyright laws. Someone could, however, take another picture of the same motel and use it without violating the copyright law.

QUESTION

I plan to sell some of my photographs to magazines as well as entering them in national contests. Some examples of these pictures are a full bench of people in Rockefeller Center Plaza; a picture of an Amish man in a Pennsylvania market; people lining the rail of a Manhattan sight seeing ferryboat; an old sea captain on the New England coast. The people in the pictures did not know I was photographing them at the time and I did not ask them for releases. Can my pictures be published even though I do not have the releases?

ANSWER

Model releases are generally required in cases where pictures are to be used for purposes of advertising or trade. If a picture is published by a photographic magazine as a contest winner or for other editorial purposes, and if the pictures do not hold a person up to ridicule or are not otherwise offensive, it is the opinion of the authors that consent of the subject should not be necessary. It is still best, of course, to have the consent.

QUESTION

I took pictures of an accident and would like to know whether, if I sell them to some interested party or an insurance company, I have the right to sell the same pictures to anyone else.

ANSWER

Assuming that you are a freelance photographer and not in the employ of any publication, when you take pictures of the accident, you have the absolute right to dispose of them under whatever terms or conditions you desire. When you wish to sell such pictures you have the option to sell either all rights to the picture, or one-time reproduction rights only, or you might make a different arrangement. Before the selling of the prints you should be sure to affix a notice of copyright on the prints, for in the situation you describe, you would not get the protection a photographer normally gets when he sells pictures to a publication. In the latter case he is protected by the copyright notice the publisher places in the magazine. Thus, if you protect yourself by appropriate copyright notice and by appropriate contract arrangement, you would have the right to sell as many prints as you may wish. On the other hand, if you sell all rights to the picture then you would have no right to resell the prints.

QUESTION

I am a professional portrait photographer of children. Do I need a release from the parents in order to enter a photograph of their child in a contest run by a photographic magazine?

ANSWER

Where you are engaged to take pictures for a fee, the relationship between you and your customer is such that while you may retain the physical possession of the negatives, you cannot do anything with them without the consent of the customer. New York and some other states would permit you to exhibit the picture on the premises of your photographic studio as samples of your work, but if the customer objects, you would have to remove the picture. Thus, the consent of the customer must be obtained before entering his picture in a contest, and the child being a minor, you would have to obtain the consent of a parent. The situation would be different in some respects if you had taken the pictures gratuitously or if they happened to be candid shots.

QUESTION

If I take a picture of a store or other private property with the consent of the owner to use it in an ad, and then I sell the picture for that purpose, is the owner of the store or other private property which was photographed entitled to any part of the profit from the sale of the photograph?

ANSWER

Since you have permission of the owner of the property and the owner has made no agreement with you regarding the division of the profit from the sale of the picture, you would not be legally obligated to give him any part of the profit. Having given his consent, the question is purely one of contract and since the owner did not protect himself he would have no claim against you.

QUESTION

I took photographs at a local summer resort for advertising purposes but did not obtain releases from the persons in the photographs. They were guests in the hotel. The owners of the resort want to use the pictures and are willing to assume full responsibility. If anyone sues me, will I be covered by such an agreement?

ANSWER

This agreement would protect you providing the resort owner is financially sound. (In several states the agreement must be made in writing.) You must remember that you will continue to be liable to the people shown in the pictures. The resort owner, by assuming responsibility, agrees to reimburse you for any damages awarded against you, but if at that time the resort is out of business or otherwise insolvent, then the agreement to indemnify you, while legally good, would naturally be a worthless piece of paper.

QUESTION

I am starting out as a candid wedding photographer. If the pictures I take at a wedding do not turn out well, can I be sued by the people who engaged me to take the pictures?

ANSWER

If you hold yourself out to be a professional photographer, competent to take pictures of a wedding and you fall down on the job, then you can be sued and held liable unless you can show you were not at fault. When you hold yourself out as a professional, the law requires that you do a good and workmanlike job. If, on the other hand, you tell your customer that you are an amateur and that you will merely do your best to do a good job, then the situation would be different and, provided the court accepts your version of the arrangement, it would not hold you liable because the pictures did not turn out well.

QUESTION

A few years ago I entered some of my pictures in a photography contest. I did not win a prize, and this year I asked the sponsor of the contest to return my pictures. I was told the prints and negatives had been destroyed six months after the contest closed in accordance with the rules announced for the contest. Why should they have the right to destroy my pictures?

ANSWER

The sponsor had a perfect right to dispose of the pictures after the period of time specified in the contest rules. The rules set forth the terms and conditions upon which pictures are submitted. You do not have to submit pictures if the rules are not to your liking. In our experience the publishers of photographic magazines always make some provision in their contest rules for the return of pictures if postage is supplied with the entry, but no one could be expected to keep mountains of pictures on hand year after year just because someone might subsequently ask for the return of his pictures. You might be interested to know that the United States Post Office Department has strict rules which must be observed by sponsors of contests who use the mails in connection with the contests.

QUESTION

I recently took some film to a local camera store for processing. Now I am told by the camera store that the processor lost my film. The pictures on the roll of film were taken at my son's birthday party, and though they aren't worth much to anyone else, they mean a lot to me. Can I sue?

ANSWER

You might sue, but even if you won your case on the ground of negligence, it would hardly be worth the trouble as a practical matter. Your problem is to establish damage, and this would be extremely difficult in your case. Nevertheless, if there were no other complications, you could receive nominal damages in an amount fixed by the judge or jury. However, you probably were given a receipt at the camera store which contained a limitation of liability to the cost of replacement of film. While the law is not too well settled on the effect of such receipts, there is at least one reported case in the lower court in New York holding that such receipt is a barrier to successful prosecution of your claim.

QUESTION

I recently took some pictures of a model who posed in the nude. I did not get a release, but the model told me when I took the pictures that I could sell them to a magazine. The magazine to whom the pictures were sent wants a written release, but the model has moved out of my town and I cannot find her. Is the release necessary?

ANSWER

The magazine is right to insist on a written release. Although many states do not require the consent of a subject in writing, the publication of a nude study without such consent is fraught with danger. The publisher as well as the photographer may be sued for invasion of privacy or libel, and no one would want to base his defense on an oral consent. In a recent New York case, a model had posed in the nude for a photographer but orally forbade him to have the picture published in any manner so that her face would show. It was established at the trial that the model had posed in the nude previously with the same restriction. The court awarded her $1500 in damages.

QUESTION

In my town a morals squad recently seized from newsstands, without a search warrant, copies of magazines that they claimed were obscene. One of the magazines was a monthly photographic publication containing two nude studies. Does the law allow local police to do this?

ANSWER

The type of seizure described in this question is a flagrant violation of constitutional rights. The Supreme Court of the United States has outlined in decisions over the past 13 years (see Chapter 5) a definition of "obscene" which, while not precise, is now fairly clear. There can be no doubt that under the tests enunciated by the court, the traditional consumer publications in the photographic field are outside the scope of any conceivable definition of obscenity. It has also been made clear, particularly in one United States Supreme Court case (*Quality of Copies of Books v. State of Kansas,* 378 U.S. 205 [1964]), that a massive seizure of books or magazines before there is an opportunity for a hearing on the question of whether the books are obscene is a violation of constitutional rights (even in a case where it turns out the books *are* obscene). The traditional rule that "prior restraint" of communications is a violation of the First Amendment (seizing books before any hearing would be a prior restraint) has however been weakened by recent decisions of the court, which permit seizure under a search warrant issued by a judge who has first seen the material and believes that there is probable cause for prosecution. (*People v. Steinberg,* 304 N.Y.S. 2d 858; *People v. Bercowitz,* 304 N.Y.S. 2d 963; *People v. Hall,* 304 N.Y.S. 2d 379; *Rage Books, Inc. v. Leary,* D.C. 301 F. Supp. 546)

QUESTION

Should a photographer incorporate?

ANSWER

This is very much a matter of general business law. The photographer is subject to the same laws which affect other business or professional men and may, of course, apply for the same benefits and advantages. The primary benefit of incorporating is generally considered to be the feature of limitation of liability. This means that if the business is unsuccessful and in debt, or otherwise incurs financial obligations, the individual stockholders need have no fear of being held liable for such obligations. Obviously, there is no sense in an amateur photographer incorporating. As to professional photographers, the advisability of incorporating would depend on the facts in each case. For example, one who works out of his home where he keeps his camera and equipment and accepts photographic assignments would appear to have no need to incorporate. On the other hand, where one or more photographers rent a studio or building under a long term lease, purchase expensive equipment under installment contracts, make other purchases on credit, have a number of employees, and do business on a large scale, it would probably be advisable to incorporate so that none of the individuals will be personally liable for the business debts if things go wrong.

There are, of course, other considerations. The problem of taxes is important and a photographer should consult his accountant or tax attorney as to the income tax rates which are applicable to each. Also, remember that aside from the original cost and legal fees, once you incorporate you must, in most states, file franchise tax returns every year and pay such tax, whether or not you do business.

Whether the benefit of limitation of personal liability outweighs some of the disadvantages will depend on each individual situation and you are urged to consult an attorney as to whether your case calls for incorporation, operating as an individual, or as a partnership.

QUESTION

What kind of insurance should a photographer carry?

ANSWER

In answering this question we are, of course, excluding any discussion of life, hospital and accident insurance. For these types of insurance the same considerations apply to the photographer and non-photographer.

As a photographer there are certain types of situations which may give rise to liability on your part and which it would be well to protect oneself against by insurance. Of course, many states now make automobile liability insurance compulsory so that if you live in one of those states, such as New York, you cannot operate a car without such insurance. However, accidents also happen in other places. If you operate a studio, you are exposed to liability for accidents on the premises, such as someone tripping over an extension cord, being burned by a light bulb, being cut by an exploding bulb, falling on a defective floor, injury while entering or leaving your premises or in countless other ways. Therefore, if you are exposed to these situations it would be most desirable for you to carry liability insurance. And don't forget that the difference in premium between a $10,000 and $50,000 policy may not be as great as you think. Juries nowadays in accident cases are known to award large amounts. If you haven't sufficient coverage your insurance company will pay up to the amount of the policy and you will have to pay the rest yourself. Therefore, don't be deluded into a false sense of security just because you have insurance. Make sure it is in a more than sufficient amount. Consult a competent insurance broker relative to your individual needs.

If you are a free lance photographer who accepts individual assignments, you may have occasion to send your pictures to a distant processor. You may have to use the mail or express. Make sure you consider insuring the film for its proper value. The premium may be inconsequential in relation to the loss you may suffer if the film is lost. Don't be penny wise and pound foolish. Use a carrier who will provide such insurance.

Suppose you have a stock of valuable pictures which you are trying to sell. Your potential customer, be it an advertising agency, publisher or other, will want you to leave your pictures for consideration. Often the pictures are lost. Insurance to cover such losses should also be considered. Since this insurance is comparatively new the premium may be high. You will have to decide whether or not it pays to carry it. Some picture agencies to whom photographers are constantly sending pictures have an arrangement for such insurance coverage at a small cost to the photographer. You should, of course, insure your equipment against loss as part of your regular personal coverage.

There are other types of insurance peculiar to photography, such as coverage for libel and violation of a person's civil rights by use of the photograph for purposes of trade or advertising without the subject's written consent. While the latter types are sometimes carried by publications, the cost for the individual photographer is likely to be prohibitive.

As the law governing photographers develops further there may be other types of situations making insurance coverage desirable.

We do not advocate that a photographer be covered against "everything." Cost is an important factor, and the decision for or against particular insurance coverage must be made on the basis of the individual situation.

QUESTION

Where a photograph is taken for use as evidence in a law suit, what records should be kept with reference to the picture?

ANSWER

Before the picture may be used in the trial, there should be preliminary proof of care and accuracy in the taking of the photograph. The photographer should have a complete record of when and where the photo was taken, under what conditions, and be able to discuss the subject of angles, light conditions and distortions.

QUESTION

May a photograph be used in evidence where the subject matter can be brought into court?

ANSWER

No. Photographs are only copies and the originals must be brought into court. A photograph of a written instrument which can be produced is therefore not admissible. On the other hand, an automobile cannot be brought into court and a photograph may be used in its place.

QUESTION

Are motion pictures showing activities of a person claiming to have been inactivated by an injury admissible in evidence?

ANSWER

Yes. As a matter of fact, insurance companies have been extremely successful in defeating disability claims based on feigned or exaggerated injuries through the use of motion pictures. Cases are not unusual where the insurance company's photographer follows a claimant for days without the subject's knowledge, taking pictures of the claimant walking, running for trains, climbing steps two at a time, lifting big objects, and other shots likely to be most embarrassing to the unsuspecting claimant at the time of the trial.

Citations

CHAPTER I
Taking the Picture

1. R.K.O. Midwest Corp. v. Berline, 51 Ohio App. 85, 199 N.E. 604 (1935)
2. N.Y. State Penal Law, Sec. 244
3. Title 18, United States Code, Sec. 474
4. Title 18, United States Code, Sec. 504
5. Public Law 79, 82d Congress, approved July 16, 1951
6. E.g., N.Y. State Penal Law, Sec. 887
7. Title 18, United States Code, Sec. 504
8. Title 50, United States Code, Sec. 45 (repealed June 25, 1948), relating to photographs of defensive installations, is covered by Sections 795-797 of Title 18
9. Title 18, United States Code, Sec. 137
10. Title 49, United States Code, Sec. 121
11. Reported in Editor & Publisher, April 17, 1954
12. Ibid.
13. See Editor & Publisher, December 28, 1963, p. 9

CHAPTER II
Right of Privacy

1. It is generally settled that only living persons have a right of privacy. See, e.g., Wyatt v. Hill's Portrait Studio, 128 N.Y.S. 247 (1911)
2. 4 Harvard Law Review 193

3. In Manola v. Stevens & Myers, N.Y. Supreme Court, reported in The New York Times, June 15, 18, 21 (1890), where an actress had been photographed surreptitiously while performing in tights, the court enjoined publication of the photographs

4. Roberson v. Rochester Folding Box Co., 171 N.Y. 538 (1902)

5. 15 Utah Rev. Stat., Secs. 103-4-7

6. Va. Code Title 8 Sec. 650 (1950)

7. Wisc. Stat. C. 348 Sec. 412 (1951)

8. See Proper on Torts

9. Lahiri v. Daily Mirror, 162 Misc. 776, 295 N.Y.S. 382 (1937)

10. Hofstadter, Development of the Right of Privacy in New York (1954)

11. Lahiri v. Daily Mirror, 162 Misc. 776, 182 (1937)

12. Koussevitzky v. Allen, Towne and Heath, 188 Misc. 479, aff'd 272 App. Div. 759 (1948)

13. Riddle v. MacFadden, 101 N.Y.S. 606 (1906), aff'd 201 N.Y. 215 (1911)

14. Booth v. Curtis Publishing Company, 15 A.D. 2d 343, 223 N.Y.S. 2d 737, aff'd 11 N.Y. 2d 907, 182 N.E. 2d 812, 228 N.Y.S. 2d 468 (1962)

15. Flores v. Mosler Safe Company, 7 N.Y. 2d 276, 196 N.Y.S. 2d 975 (1959)

16. Gautier v. Pro Football, Inc., 340 N.Y. 254 (1952)

17. Sutton v. Hearst Corporation, 277 App. Div. 155 (1950)

18. See Leverton v. Curtis Publishing Company, 192 F. 2d 974 (3rd Cir. 1951)

19. Sweenek v. Pathé News Inc., 16 F. Supp. 746 (D.C.N.Y. 1936)

20. Humiston v. Universal Film Mfg. Co., 189 App. Div. 467 (1919)

21. Jenkins v. Dell Publishing Co., 251 F. 2d 487 (C.A. Pa. 1958)

22. Sidis v. F-R Pub. Corp., 113 F. 2d 806 (2d Cir. 1940), cert. den. 61 S.Ct. 393 (1940)

23. Wilson v. Brown, 189 Misc. 79 (1947)

24. 202 F. 2d 866 (1952), cert. den. 346 U.S. 816

25. See Nimmer, The Right of Publicity, 1954, 19 Law & Contemp. Prob. 203

26. Continental Optical C. v. Reed, 119 Ind. App. 643, 86 N.E. 2d 306 (1949)

27. Lahiri v. Daily Mirror, 162 Misc. 776, 882 (1937)
28. 101 N.Y.S. 2d 532 (1951), 278 App. Div. 964, aff'd 303 N.Y. 759
29. Leverton v. Curtis Publishing Company, 192 Fed. 2d 974 (3d Cir. 1951)
30. Gill v. Curtis Pub. Co., 239 P.2d 630 (Cal. 1952)
31. See, e.g., Kelly v. Johnson Publishing Co., 325 P.2d 659 (Cal. App. 1959)
32. See Footnote 1, also annotation in 14 A.L.R. 2d 757 n.
33. Lawrence v. Ylla, 184 Misc. 807
34. Ibid.
35. 176 Misc. 714, 28 N.Y.S. 2d 811 (1941). There was a decision in New York that a gratuitous consent could be revoked at any time, but it is not expected that the courts would reach such a result where the photographer has taken action in reliance upon the gratuitous consent
36. Buscelle v. Conde Nast Publ., 173 Misc. 674, 19 N.Y.S. 2d 129 (1940)
37. Sidney v. A.S. Beck Shoe Corp., 153 Misc. 166, 274 N.Y.S. 559 (1934)
38. Russel v. Marboro Books, 18 Misc. 2d 166, 183 N.Y.S. 2d 8 (1959)
39. Carlson v. Hillman Periodicals, Inc., 3 A.D. 2d 987, 163 N.Y.S. 2d 21 (1957), reversing 157 N.Y.S. 2d 88

CHAPTER III
Who Owns the Picture

1. White Studio Inc. v. Dreyfoos, 156 App. Div. 762 (N.Y.) (1913); Lumiere v. Robertson-Cole Distributing Corp., 280 Fed 550 (2d Cir.), cert. den. 259 U.S. 583 (1922)
2. Colten v. Jacques Marchais, Inc., 61 N.Y.S. 2d 269 (N.Y.) (1946)
3. Hochstadter v. H. Tarr, Inc., 68 N.Y.S. 2d 762 (1947)
4. Avedon v. Exstein, 141 F. Supp. 278 (S.D.N.Y. 1956)
5. See note in Harvard Law Review, January, 1957, for an opinion that the court should have allowed evidence of trade usage to be introduced
6. Press Publishing Co. v. Falk, 59 Fed. 324 (1894)
7. Thayer v. Worcester Post Co., 284 Mass. 160 (1933)
8. Young v. J. J. Hickerson, Inc., 159 N.Y.S. 2d 612, rev'd NYLJ, Sept. 12, 1957 (App. Term)

9. Lawrence v. Ylla, 184 Misc. 807 (N.Y.)
10. Ibid.

CHAPTER IV

Loss of and Damage to Film

1. 228 N.Y.S. 2d 330
2. 12 N.Y.2d 301, 239 N.Y.S.2d 337, 189 N.E.2d 693
3. Goor v. Navilio, 177 Misc. 970 (N.Y. 1941)
4. Nathan v. Fotoshop, 5th Dist. Munc. Ct., Manhattan (N.Y.) (1951)
5. Lake v. Railway Express Agency, 98 N.Y.S. 2nd 202, 277 App. Div. 853 (1950)
6. Wamsley v. Atlas Steamship Co., 50 App. Div. 199 (N.Y.) (1900)

CHAPTER V

The Nude in Photography and the Law of Obscenity

1. Title 18, United States Code, Sec. 334
2. N.Y. State Penal Law, Sec. 235.—235.22
3. N.Y. State Penal Law, Sec. 235.21
4. Kingsley Pictures Corp. v. Regents, 360 U.S. 684 (1959)
5. Commercial Pictures Corp. v. Regents, 346 U.S. 587 (1954)
6. Superior Films, Inc. v. Dep't of Education, 346 U.S. 587 (1954)
7. Gelling v. Texas, 343 U.S. 960 K(1952)
8. 354 U.S. 476 (1957); See also Alberts v. California, 354 U.S. 476 (1957)
9. 370 U.S. 478
10. See, e.g., Peiple v. Richmond County News, Inc., 9 N.Y. 2d 578 (1961)
11. People v. Finkelstein, 114 N.Y.S. 2d 810 (1952)
12. People v. Gonzales, 107 N.Y.S. 2d 968 (1951)
13. People v. Rosenzweig, 107 N.Y.S. 2d 968 (1951)
14. People v. Finkelstein, 107 N.Y.S. 2d 968 (1951)
15. Jacobellis v. State of Ohio, 378 U.S. 184 (1964)

CHAPTER VI

Copyright

1. 13 World Book Encyclopedia 5582 (1938 ed.)

2. 38th Cong., 2d Sess., Ch. 126. See Copyright Enactments (Copyright Office, Bull. No. 3, rev.) p. 34

3. Although state protection for unpublished works is sometimes based on statute (e.g. Calif. Civil Code, Sec. 980 [a], it is nevertheless referred to by general usage as "common law copyright." The term "statutory copyright," according to accepted usage, refers to the federal Copyright Act, 17 U.S.C. 1 et seq. See Nimmer on Copyright 31, fn. (1964)

4. 376 U.S. 225 (1964)

5. See Capitol Records, Inc. v. Greatest Records, Inc., 142 U.S.P.Q. 109 (Sup. N.Y. Co., 1964); Columbia Broadcasting System, Inc. v. Documentaries Unlimited, Inc., 42 Misc. 2d 723 (1964); Flamingo Telefilm Sales, Inc. v. United Artists Corp., 141 U.S.P.Q. 461 (Sup., N.Y. Co., 1964)

6. Compco Corp. v. Day-Brite Lighting Co., 376 U.S. 234 (1964), decided together with Sears Roebuck & Co. v. Stiffel Co., supra, on the basis of the same newly enunciated rule of law, also involved a lamp.

7. 17 U.S.C. §2

8. Lumiere v. Pathé Exchange, Inc., 275 Fed. 428 (1921)

9. Washingtonian Publishing Co. v. Pearson, 300 U.S. 30 (1939)

10. Where the publisher acquires only limited reproduction rights, he often requires a specific consent to secure copyright in his name as part of the contract of purchase. This is one way to show, if necessary, that the publisher's general copyright notice in his magazine or book covered the particular photograph, thus preserving the copyright for the photographer

11. See American Visuals Corporation v. Holland, 239 F.2d 740 (2d Cir. 1956)

12. Gross v. Seligman, 212 F. 2d 930 (1914)

13. Bolton v. Aldin, 56 LJB 120 (1895)

CHAPTER VII
Libel by Photograph

1. Burton v. Crowell Publishing Co., 81 Fed. 154 (2d Cir. 1936)

2. This is usually accomplished by statute. See N.Y. State Penal Law Sec. 1342

3. Van Wiginton v. Pulitzer Pub. Co., 218 Fed. 795 (8th Cir. 1914)
4. Sydney v. MacFadden News Publishing Corp., 242 N.Y. 208 (1926)
5. Zbyszko v. N.Y. American, 239 N.Y.S. 411 (1930)
6. Reported in Editor & Publisher, Aug. 1, 1953, p. 40
7. Jackson v. Consumers Publications, Inc., 11 N.Y.S. 2d 462 (1932)
8. Meyers v. Afro-American Pub. Co., Inc., 5 N.Y.S. 2d 223 (1938)
9. Peck v. Tribune Co., 214 U.S. 185 (1909)
10. See Liccione v. Collier, 117 N.Y.S. 639 (1909). The trial court was reversed on other grounds

CHAPTER VIII

Photographs as Evidence

1. Cowley v. People, 83 N.Y. 464 (1881)
2. Alberti v. New York L.E. & W.R.R. Co., 118 N.Y. 77 (1889)
3. Dresch v. Elliott, 137 App. Div. 252 (N.Y.) (1914)
4. Fearon v. New York Life Ins. Co., 162 App. Div. 560 (N.Y.) (1914)
5. Gibson v. Gunn, 206 App. Div. 464 (N.Y.) (1923)
6. Cirello v. Metropolitan Express Co., 88 N.Y.S. 932 (1904)
7. Cozzens v. Higgins, 3 Keyes 206, 33 How. Pr. 436 (N.Y.) (1886)
8. Boyarsky v. G.A. Zimmerman Corp., 240 App. Div. 361 (N.Y.) (1934)

CHAPTER IX

Photography — Business, Art or Profession

1. City of New Orleans v. Robira, 42 La. Ann. 1098 (1890)
2. Story v. Walker, 11 Lea 515 (Tenn.) (1883)
3. Cecil v. Inland Rev. Com., 36 Times Law Reports 164 (1919)
4. People v. Cross and Brown Co., 232 App. Div. 587, 251 N.Y.S. 138 (1931)
5. People ex rel Tower v. State Tax Com., 282 N.Y. 407 (1940)
6. Buehman v. Bechtel, 114 P. 2nd 227 (Arizona)
7. Territory v. Kraft, 33 Hawaii 397 (1935)
8. Wright v. Wiles, 173 Tenn. 334 (1938)
9. Schlesinger v. City of Atlanta, 161 Ga. 148 (1925)
10. State v. Cromwell, 9 N. Car. 2nd 914 (1943)

Index

Date Due

	7 1996			

3 5282 00298 0871